CLOSE ENCOUNTER: MEMOIR MOMENTS OF A PROFESSIONAL FOOTBALL PLAYER

Charles Ray Jefferson

Close Encounter: Memoir Moments of A Professional Football Player

ISBN 13: 9798566101750

Printed in the United States of America

Makeover of Memoirs:

Be the first to write a review and to share your thoughts on this awesome book. After playing football at McNeese State University in the 1970s, I went on to play for the Denver Broncos and Houston Oilers. God willing, this book will be one of the best football memoirs ever written, and will be produced and released as a movie portraying my amazing life.

I dedicate this book to family, friends, fans, and my legacy.

1975-78

FIRST TEAM ALL LOUISIANA 1976

THREE-TIME ALL SLC FIRST TEAM

20 CAREER INTERCEPTIONS

1970

ALL DECK TEAM

McNeese State University

HALL OF FAME

INDUCTEE

A Legacy of Achievement

Table of Contents

Acknowledgments

Many people have contributed to this book.

I would like to express my deepest gratitude to Melissa Eastin, Emily Ward, Ashley Michel, Kathy Rome, Pastor Joe Connerly Jr., Angelo Sideris, Alex Bourgeois, Latrenda Jefferson, Brenita Pelichet, Willie Russell, Patti Threatt, and Marisha Mathis. I want to thank you all for your help with research, referrals, and editorial assistance.

Thank you to my wife, Deborah Jefferson, for your patience and understanding that kept me focused and driven. Your support helped me finish the course. Thank you for the wise counsel and suggestions.

Also, thanks to the countless fans and friends who have helped open my eyes and ears to new truths in life.

CHARLES
JEFFERSON
37

Prologue

There are some things that occurred in my life during the process of writing this book:

1. Diagnosed with pulmonary embolism
2. The great flood of 2016
3. Helped my father rebuild his flooded home
4. My wife and I retired from your jobs
5. Mother-in-law turned eighty-two years old
6. Son Brandon got married to Melinda
7. I turned sixty years old
8. Daughter, D'andra, brought her first home
9. Grandchildren celebrated their birthdays: Aerion turned eleven, Erin turned nine, Eric III turned eight
10. Son Bryan got engaged to Athaliah
11. Niece Elizabeth Porche turned twenty years old

12. Dad, Saymon Jefferson Sr., turned ninety-three years old
13. I was named to McNeese State ALL- 75th Anniversary football team
14. The loss of a dear friend, Jeffery Lendo Sr.
15. Brandon and Melinda were expecting their first child and hosted a gender-reveal party and played Wheels or Heels
16. Sister-in-law Yvette Henderson turned fifty years old
17. Granddaughter Brooklyn soon to be due in July 2018
18. Son Bryan got married to Athealiah
19. Niece Marisa Danielle Jefferson got married
20. The Loss of a brother in-law, Eddie C. Henderson (A.K.A. "Man").
21. The loss of my baby sister Carolyn Yvette Jefferson Porche.

More memorable moments of my life are uploaded on my YouTube channel, Boh_Chas_Jefferson or search "Charles Ray Jefferson".

The Call

On an August afternoon, I was on my way to visit my father, picking up the dinner he asked for. Shortly after I reached my destination, I was exiting my vehicle when my phone rang. The incoming call was from a 337 area code, which meant the call was coming from Lake Charles, LA. So, I answered the phone with precaution. It was Matthew Bonnette, Sports Information Director at McNeese State University. He said, "Is this Charles Jefferson?" I said, "Yes, What's this all about?"

He paused for a moment to gather his thoughts. What happened next blew me away and made my day. "Charles, you have been nominated for McNeese State University Football Hall of Fame, class of 2014." This was an extremely emotional moment for me. All I could say afterward was, "thank you, Matthew, for the great news!" Before ending the call, he stated that he would send all the details regarding the ceremony in about a week. "See you and your family in September, Charles."

It was time to notify my family and friends of the good news following what I deem as "the call." I told my father first. He was thrilled. He felt that I had indeed earned it. I then told my wife, Deborah, who also offered much congratulatory remarks and praise on my accomplishments. Next, I informed our kids Eric, Brandon, Bryan, and D'andra, who were all proud of me. I then notified each of my siblings to share the good news about my induction. Everyone was excited about the opportunity and was looking forward to the ceremony.

It was awesome news. It felt bittersweet, but many people wondered why. It was because my mother had already passed away to be with her Creator. She was the one person who had been there for me to protect, teach, mentor, motivate, and so much more. I know she would have been tremendously proud of me and all of my accomplishments.

The Selection of My Name

Who had the last word? My mother, of course! The story was later told to me by my father and siblings. My mother said she would name her son after Ray Charles Robinson: the great singer, songwriter, and pianist if God gave her another son. He was sometimes referred to as "the genius". Can you imagine that? Although it didn't exactly work the way she had hoped, it came exceedingly close. I wholeheartedly believe my father had something to say about the final decision of my name. Although he denies it to this day. Truth be known, I'm glad it turned out the way it did. I like my name much better. Before I transition from this story, I would like to interject a teachable moment from my mother at the age of six. My mother, who was an intelligent devout Christian, taught my siblings and I sound and strong Christian values to live by from the benefits of hard work. She also taught us how to treat others with honor, dignity, and love. She taught us that we should treat others in a way that we would want to be treated. As the reading continues, you will learn many more qualities about my mother.

In Honor of My Big Brother, Saymon Jr.

Saymon Jr. was the firstborn to Arcenia and Saymon Jefferson Sr. I looked up to my big brother for love, respect, and protection. That's what most younger siblings would look for in an older brother or sister. I couldn't have asked for a better one. He was someone I shared a bunk bed with and didn't mind teaching me about the birds and bees. My brother was smart, determined, driven, and a well-thought-out person. Most importantly, I saw him as someone with a passion to give back. He loved helping others no matter the circumstances were. His profession as a Social Worker for forty-plus years has stood the test of time.

Thank you, for being not only my big brother but also a father-figure growing up.

Little Bro

In Honor of My Big Sister, Gertie

The second oldest born to Arcenia and Saymon Jefferson Sr. is my sister, Gertie. I thought it was cool to have a big sister as a kid. She was sincere, nice, sweet, and a warm, virtuous woman of God. She would always show me lots of affection in my youth. She also taught me life lessons just like my mother. As time passed I couldn't help but notice how much my sister Gertie had become like my mother in all many ways. She became a great cook, excellent homemaker/caretaker, and a wonderful singer—all thanks to my mother. Thank you, Sis, for all your love and support.

Little Bro

In Honor of My Little Sister, Belvin

The fourth child to be born to Saymon and Arcenia Jefferson Sr. is Belvin. In my humble opinion, growing up with Belvin was an adventure. She is smart, witty, feisty, and she loved to sing. Singing was merely one of her many gifts. She was also very funny. She may have inherited that from our father- I hope she does not mind me saying. Belvin, being two years younger than me would try her best to keep up with me. I had a great deal of energy in my younger years. It was somewhat difficult for her to keep up at times. Today she is known as the family comedian in a wholesome way. However, growing up with Belvin was quite an honor.

Big Bro

In Honor of My Baby Sister, Carolyn

Carolyn is the fifth born to Arcenia and Saymon Jefferson Sr. In my humble opinion, I describe her as smart, charming, shy and beautiful. She is someone who could light up a room with just a smile. These are only a few of her attributes. Growing up, she would offer me support and love no matter what decisions I made rather good, bad, or indifferent. I will always be grateful to her for that. As the youngest, she constantly received love, protection, and nurturing from everyone.

Big Bro

Timeline Leading up to The Barber Shooting

Early one Wednesday morning, just like any other summer day during the life and times of Charles Ray Jefferson, my dad had already left for work leaving behind a wife, two sons, and two daughters. Several hours later, I would be awakened by mom. It was a day filled with excitement going to visit Mr. Joe for a hair- cut. It wasn't long before my mom and I would leave home for Reynolds' Barbershop, unaware of what imminent danger lay ahead for us. We continued after about a ten-minute drive, we arrived. Mom would always park on the lot adjacent to the building. Once we arrived, mom and I got out of the car walked in together in lock-step. One other thing of note; I remember the front entrance door was open on arrival that day.

The Barber that Saved My Life

It was July 14, 1960. I was three years old. I will try and explain what happened that morning some 59 years ago at Reynolds' barbershop. Mr. Joe Davis was considered by many to be one of the finest barbers in town. However, my mother and I could have never imagined what would happen on this particular visit. The day began like any other day that I would go to the barber. My mother and I left home and took our usual route to the shop. We always arrived around 10:30 a.m. But no matter what time of day, I was happy to always see Mr. Joe. He wasn't just a great a barber. He was also smart and witty. In other words, he made me laugh a lot at the age of 3. My mother and I greeted Mr. Joe by saying "Good morning Mr. Joe." We then greeted the others in the shop before taking our seats on the wall alongside the windows.

Shortly after taking our seats, I remember Mr. Joe telling my mother that it wouldn't be long before I was up. Mom resumed reading her newspaper as she always did. There was a television that I always enjoyed watching while I waited for my turn. It wasn't long before Mr. Joe finished the customer before me. He took a short bathroom break and upon his return, he called me to his chair. My mom walked me over and she assisted Mr. Joe with getting me into the chair before each cut. Then he would pull out this special board that I would sit on while he cut my hair. This was a rite of passage for me. Previously my mom would have to hold me while I got my hair cut but since I was older, I was able to sit alone like the older kids. I thought that I was cool.

It was not even 10 minutes after he got me situated in the chair and when all hell broke loose. A man appeared at the doorway asking to see Mr. Joe. An argument ensued between the two men. I was right in the midst of it. Next, to everyone's shock and horror the man pulled out a gun and began shooting at Mr. Joe. I was injured in my upper left arm during the shooting. Amid the gunfire, Mr. Joe had the presence of mind to spin my chair around for added protection which saved my life. I may have been mortally wounded if it wasn't for Mr. Joe's heroic efforts. And yes! My mother was right there and never left my side.

I had never heard my mom scream as loudly as she did that morning. it was so intense. She could have erupted a volcano. After the gunfire stopped my mother rushed over to me not knowing her baby boy had been hit in the upper left arm by a stray bullet. She took me in her arms and tried to console me as I bled from my gunshot wound. We waited there several minutes for the ambulance to arrive. I vividly remember Mr. Joe lying face up in a pool of blood. He was bleeding profusely from his chest, neck, mouth, and ears. Mr. Joe Davis was transported and admitted to the hospital with several bullet wounds. His condition was later described as critical.

Mr. Joe remained in the hospital for approximately six months before he returned to his craft of cutting hair some several years later. Mr. Joe met a man by the name of "Jesus" and was saved following the encounter. He was later called to preaching the gospel of Christ for the rest of his life. Many decades later I asked my father Saymon Jefferson Sr. to explain what he knew about Mr. Joe Davis. I learned that first that he graduated from McKinley high school; he was a fighter/boxer, a very good one at that. He was also a certified barber and last, but not least, he was married with a wonderful family. Joe Davis had a lot of great traits and these were just a few to speak of.

Next, my father gave me a little history of Reynolds' Barbershop where the shooting took place. Reynolds' Barbershop was the top negro barbershop in Baton Rouge, LA. After young black barbers graduated from school, they would seek out for an opportunity to work at Reynolds' Barber Shop. This was the place that one would want to start before branching out on their own.

Here's what happened, my father said that Mr. Reynolds was a highly respected, well-liked, and hardworking man. The negro gunmen Virdure told the detectives that he took a beating on Monday night by the hands of Joe Davis. That is what set the whole shooting ordeal into motion. Virdure was sentenced to eight years in Angola prison after he pled guilty to counts of attempted murder.

Bible verses to live by

- Put on the whole armour of God, that ye may be able to stand against the wiles of the devil.-Ephesians 6:11
- I will sing unto the Lord, because he hath dealt bountifully with me.-Psalm 13: 6
- Be ye angry, and sin not: let not the sun go down upon your wrath-Ephesians 4:26
- If any man serve me, let him follow me; and where I am, there shall also my servant be: if any man serve me, him will my Father honour.-John 12:26

Foul Play: The Lifeguard that Almost Drowned Me

It was July of 1973. The day started off like any other summer day. My friends and I decided to go to the public pool for a swim. We were playing and hanging out doing things that boys did and also talking to some of the girls. Shortly after, my boys and I decided that it was time to go to the deeper end of the pool where all the action was. The deeper end of the pool was 10 feet deep. You had to be an experienced swimmer to get in. I had lots of experience in swimming even though I was only thirteen. This was because of some amazing swimmers that I looked up to like Robbie Collins aka Bo Rob, Asberry Doyle aka Bootsy, and last but not least Gregory Doyle aka Zeke.

I finally got in despite my rocky start. I'm very grateful for their help that day. I would not be the swimmer that I am if it wasn't for them. They taught me many techniques like freestyle swimming, breaststroke, backstroke, diving, dog-paddling, and underwater swimming. Finally, the day arrived for me to be able to swim in any part of the pool. First, I had to complete a three-part test. The lifeguard instructed me to enter from the shallow end-which was three feet, for the first part of the test. He then told me to swim to the other end of the pool and freestyle back without stopping. I did just as he had instructed and passed.

Next, he wanted me to get out of the pool, onto the bank walk down to the deep end, get in, and swim across and back freestyle without stopping. I did what he asked and made it to the next phase. Last, it was time for the third and final phase. The lifeguard directed me to the highest diving board, told me to walk slow, and to jump into the pool. Following his instructions, I went down to the bottom of the pool, touched it, and came back to the surface. I made a strong swim back to the bank. I was then greeted by the head lifeguard. He told me that I passed the swimming test and congratulated me.

Several of my peers came over to congratulate me. During all the excitement, I had no idea what near-death tragedy awaited me. But, for now, all things were great. I was having a blast with my friends-board diving and cannonball runs off the high low boards. After about an hour of fun in the deep end, it was time to head back to the shallow waters for some quiet time and relaxation with the girls.

Before I left, I just had to dive off the low board one more time. However, before I could get back to where I started that day in the shallow end, I had to get past the lifeguard who was known as "Ring Eye." I had been warned by my peers to avoid Ring Eye. He was someone you didn't want to be on the wrong side of. His temperament was unpredictable at times. Sure, enough it wasn't long before I encountered the unpredictable temperament of Ring Eye on my way back to the shallow waters. He was about 17 years old and physically intimidating. I remember that much about him very well. Ring Eye suddenly grabbed me by my upper torso as I was swimming carefree to the shallow end.

I remember him dunking me in and out of the water several times with great force. All I could do was fight for dear life at that moment. I managed to break free from the total chaos and from the maniac called Ring Eye by the grace of God. I was able to swim back to shallow waters after breaking free. I thought lifeguards were supposed to save lives, not take them. I had just stared death in the face once again, due to the rage of Ring Eye. Guys like Ring Eye gave lifeguards a bad name. It was not long before my friends came over to offer words of comfort and support. Unfortunately, things happened so fast that day there was nothing they could do to help.

Afterward, one of my friends suggested I report him to management for disciplinary actions. Ring Eye was given a three-day suspension without pay for his actions against me, for that I was grateful. It took me about three days to recover from the terrifying ordeal. My friends suggested I report him to management for disciplinary actions.

Lessons from this tale are listed below in a question format below. See if you can fill in the blanks.

What makes lifeguards mad?

____

____

____

Can you drown in a swimming pool?

____

____

____

How many kids die in a pool every year?

____

____

____

What is the leading cause for drowning?

____

____

____

Why are lifeguards put in place?

____

____

____

Grandparents: Teachable Moments

I spent many long, hot summers away from home with my paternal grandparents, Joe and Augustine Jefferson. They lived in Cloutierville, Louisiana. It was a small town just north of Alexandria, Louisiana. It was quite a challenge to not have my parents around for the first visit. I never really knew what to expect from my grandparents. I guess you could say I just went with the flow. I was a young lad that wanted to prove to myself that I could bear the distance between my other siblings and me.

I must admit that I cried often in the beginning. I soon realized there would be places to go, people to see, things to do, and life lessons to be learned from both grandparents. I knew that it wouldn't be easy while I was there. I still remember the countless rules and guidelines my grandparents had during those visits. My grandfather, known as Pop-Pop Joe, stood about five feet seven inches tall from what I can remember. He weighed about 160 pounds. He had a dark complexion. He was a farmer, a builder, a great teacher, a leader, a loving husband, and a father. I can remember a few things he taught me when I would go visit.

He taught me much about people, places, and things. He taught me to always respect my elders and to always finish what I start. He also taught me to understand what I was encountering before I agreed to it or made a final decision. He taught me about operating his farm equipment. He taught me how to drive his red and white farm tractor. He taught me how to crank up his work truck. He taught me how to catch fish, how to use hand tools, and the proper way to care for them. Last, he also taught me how to identify wild animals lurking in the bush and to stay vigilant. He taught me well.

Thank you, Pop-Pop Joe

My Grandmother

My grandmother stood about five feet four inches tall, weighed about 140 pounds, and had beautiful long black hair and brown eyes. She was smart and loved to read novels. She was an excellent home provider and a wonderful wife and mother who loved her family. She was also a God-fearing woman who loved her church family. It was quite obvious to me by the amount of time she spent there. She taught me many things about life: how to retrieve eggs from a chicken nest; how to distribute chicken feed in equal parts; how to use a washboard for cleaning clothes; how to use a hot iron on clothes; She always told me to practice personal hygiene and that it needed to be done daily. Additionally, she taught me how to wring the neck of a chicken. A little harsh, I know. There were other ways to do this. However, that was the option she chose to apply. We had to eat. She also showed me how to bleed it, gut it, boil it, and pluck it. In the grand scheme of things, something has to die so that we might live. That was my grandma Augustine, who was quite a woman in her own right!

Thank God Almighty for my grandparents and the years I spent with them learning real-life lessons. I cannot help but think of how proud they would be to know the man I have become. Again, to my grandparents, I just want to say thank you for the life lessons you taught me that I would use for a lifetime.

Sincere thoughts,

Grandson

Bad Influences

The summer I masqueraded as a Thief

Someone later asked "How did you start and why did you stop?" It was the summer of 1966 when I met this character by the name of Gin Tee. Gin Tee had a reputation of being the neighborhood thief. He brought food commodities such as candies, cookies, you name he had it. Some would say he was so good at his craft he could undress you from the crown of your head to the sole of your feet in minutes. I remember as I watched him, I often wondered how he was able to do what he did. Until one day, he showed my friends and me how it was done. He told us the two key things to look for. One was to find the weakest link in the store, be it female or male. The other was to notice the mirrors' positions in the store.

After learning these valuable lessons, I decided to case out my first store. Gin Tee informed me that Rabello's was an easy target to hit for a beginner like me. I decided that would be my first hit. After about a week of casing out the store, I decided on a date and began to prepare. I was completely stressed out as I thought about it the night before. I was going against all the principles I had been taught by my parents. I was still determined to go through with it. I was deceived into believing that I was not doing anything wrong because I wasn't going to get caught. The day finally came when I was going to make my first attempt at stealing food commodities such as candies, cakes, cookies, and so on. I did everything that Gin Tee told me to, and it was very successful. It was like taking candy from a baby.

With this new rush of success, I felt that I was invincible and had to do it again and again. It wasn't until my fifth or six attempts that things took a turn for the worst. I became so emboldened that I didn't listen to the advice that was given by Gin Tee. I felt it didn't matter who was in the store. I believed that I would still be able to pull off my masquerade of thievery. As I attempted to steal for the last time, I was caught red-handed with a hand in the cookie jar. I felt a firm grip on the back of my shirt collar. It was the store manager.

He said, "son come with me. I'm going to call your brother and let him know what you have done." He pulled me behind the store counter and told me to wait here. He also reminded me of what I had done and informed me that there could be repercussions for my actions.

As I sat behind the counter waiting there so patiently, I could only think about the punishment and shame that awaited me. Upon my brother's arrival, the store manager informed my brother of what had happened. He assured my brother that I was a good kid and that I had been misled, tricked, and duked. We walked back home in dead silence after I was released into the custody of my big brother. All I could think about was the punishment that I would receive from my parents as I walked home.

To my surprise, my brother didn't mention it to my parents as we entered the house. Before going to bed, my brother talked to me and got my side of the story. He told me never to do it again. My brother has still never said anything about it to anyone. It has remained our secret even after fifty-plus years.

The lessons from this tale are listed in a question format. See if you can answer them.

At what age is a child most influenced?

____

____

How can you avoid bad company?

____

____

How do strangers influence us?

____

____

How can you avoid making bad decisions?

____

____

A Story About Winning

Coach Hogan was a basketball coach and Physical Education teacher. He stood about six feet seven inches tall and was someone I respected and admired. He was always there to lend a hand whenever I needed one on the basketball court or in the classroom. He taught me how to play checkers—a lesson that I have carried throughout my life. He was known for being the best Checkers player on campus. Over time, I watched him play and beat opponents over and over again. He was unbeatable. I tried to beat him as well, but I failed like everyone else. However, it wasn't enough to convince me to stop trying. My mom and dad had instilled how to be a winner no matter the odds in me. At that moment, I just wanted to prove to Coach Hogan that he could be beaten. Over the next two weeks, I would watch and learn from him. I would also practice with kids in my neighborhood for a shot at the master.

Finally, the time came for me to challenge Coach Hogan. I asked him if he would play against me with the best two out of three games as the winner. He said, "of course." I made sure there were people around to witness the big matchup. Everything was set. We had bragging rights on the line—it was the student versus the master! I had been waiting and preparing for this moment for a long time. I suddenly made several daring moves and surprisingly won about twenty minutes into the first game.

We took a break after the first game to refresh before the next one. Coach Hogan pulled out a few tricks of his own and won the second game. I knew I had to change my strategy and be at my best if I wanted to win the third and final game. It was intense from the start. Thirty minutes into the game, I held my position strong. Ultimately, Coach made a few bad moves. I was able to capitalize and finish the game with yet another win. Lesson learned: you must practice long and hard before you can play the game of checkers well.

Thank you, Coach Hogan, for your patience, understanding, and mentorship you shared with me as a teacher and as a coach.

The Climb: A Landmark Moment

It was middle to late September of 1970. I met up with some friends at BREC City Park for a friendly, hard-hitting game of football. I really didn't think much of it at the time. Little did I know my Creator was preparing me for many blessings to come as it pertained to the game of football. From time to time, my mother would say, "Son, anything in life worth having is worth waiting for. There will be times when you will be tested to exercise your faith." To this very day, those words from my mother still hold true.

So, we warmed up for the game at the park. All of a sudden, I heard a disturbance coming from the northeast corner of the park. So, I stopped my warm-ups to check it out. I arrived at the commotion to find about a half dozen people watching and cheering for a man as he attempted to climb a twelve-foot landmark from the Spanish American War. At first glance, I wasn't sure how long the landmark had been there since it was the first time I had laid eyes on it. I asked someone in the crowd what was happening. They informed me that the man was trying to climb the landmark. He ran towards it at a fast pace and leaped onto it, making his way up to the top.

The landmark stood about twelve feet tall and nine to ten feet wide. I found it somewhat disturbing and perplexing that this man would be attempting this feat all by himself. I must admit I was impressed by his actions. A couple of friends and I decided to stay and try once the crowd began to vacate the scene. *Why not?* We thought. We all gave it several tries, and we all failed. The climb did not seem as difficult while standing amongst the crowd. Boy, was I wrong.

The landmark presented a new challenge that I wanted to conquer. During my spare time, over the next two or three weeks, I devised a strategy on how to achieve the feat. I started with the "big four" (prayer, patience, faith, and drive). For some odd ball reason, I felt I had inside me what it took to conquer this statue. The big four played a vital role in the process. The first week consisted of many trials and errors. Nevertheless, I stayed the course since there were things concerning my technique that needed to be adjusted.

I was beginning to think I was in over my head and wanted to walk away after a few more failures . I felt like quitting because of previous failures. But there was something inside of me that would not accept failure as the final answer. I decided to go to the park and try again on a Friday afternoon around 3:30. After warm-ups, I attempted and failed again. But the second attempt that day was the moment I had been waiting for. I stood about eight feet behind the landmark. I was about to conquer.

After a brief moment of silence, I took off running straight at it. Then upon approach, I leaped up onto it and proceeded to climb to the top. The first words that I uttered were "I did it." I felt like I needed to succeed a couple of more times before calling for witnesses. The next day I had a few friends meet me at the city park around 10:00 a.m. to prove my point. I was ready after a short warm-up session.

The time had come for me to put up or shut up. No one there knew I had already made the climb the day before. Oh boy, they were in for a surprise. As they stood there and watched, I took off running directly towards the landmark. Upon reaching the base of it, I stopped and exploded onto it like a cannonball as I climbed to the top. I could hear the cheers coming from my peers. I truly liked the cheers and the way it made me feel. Once again, I had accomplished something that I set out to do.

"Jesus said unto him if thou canst believe, All things are possible to him that believeth." (Mark 9: 23)

Meeting Brother Paul and Gaining Weight for A Purpose

I was faced with many more challenges as my life continued. I was around fourteen years old when my father decided to relocate his family to North Baton Rouge. He was able to move his family to a bigger home in Fairfield Park. I was not at all that excited about the move at first. I was leaving behind so many friends whom I thought I would never see again. That's life. Friends come and go, do they not? There would be new things to come: new neighbors, new friends, playgrounds, girls, and a new Junior High School. I can remember being enrolled in Istrouma Junior High. It was sometimes a little strenuous and testy for me due to integration. I faced a few challenges in the classroom, as well as on the football field, basketball court, and track field. I learned to deal with each one of them daily.

I recall a moment when the boys and I were at my place playing a game of tackle football when, all of a sudden, I saw my mother standing there, peeping through the window at me. It wasn't the peeping or staring that bothered me; it was what she said to me later that evening that did. She simply stated to me, "Son, I stood at the window watching you play, and you looked so skinny standing next to those boys outside." I was shocked to hear those words roll out of my mother's lips. I thought I was a pretty buff dude for my age, but for some reason, my mother saw it differently. I had a plan to turn a negative point-of-view into a positive one.

Not too long afterward, I met a guy at the local 7-Eleven store in the neighborhood. His name was Paul. He stood about five feet six inches tall and weighed about 135 pounds. I know it's strange, but this guy's physique caught my eye. His neck, chest, arms, and legs were all well developed. He reminded me of a bodybuilder, and I liked what I saw in him. Before he left, I asked him if he was a body-bodybuilder. He replied, "Why do you ask?" I stated, "You look like a bodybuilder, that's all. I'm looking for somebody who can help me build my physique. Thought you might be the guy." He shared with me that he lived one street over from where I lived. He suggested that I stop by one afternoon and look around. He offered to show me a few things that might help with my physical development. I quickly said, "I'll be there."

After several days it was time to pay Paul a visit. My goal that day was to find out how he managed to build such an impressive physique. I arrived at his home and knocked on the front door. He answered and asked me to come in. I did. "Let me show you around the place. By the way, my parents are not here, so relax." So, I did just that during the house tour. He took me outside to the garage and opened the door after looking around. I stood there in amazement and disbelief at what I saw for a moment. There were weights everywhere! There were dumbbells, a weight bench, Olympic-style weights, and much more. Then he said to me, "Brother Charles, if you want a physique like mine, you have to put the time in."
"Great, how soon can we start?" I asked.

We agreed to start the following Friday. This was something I really wanted badly. I was willing and able to put in the time to get the results I was looking for. Going into it, all I could think about were the comments my mother made about me being skinny. They did not sit well with me.

Friday finally arrived. I went to meet up with Paul for my first official weight workout. I had no idea that he would put me through one hell of a warm-up regiment. It was unlike anything I had ever experienced before in my life. I realized that it was just the beginning of something I wanted to do for a long time. Once the warm-up sessions were complete, it was time to get down to the meat of the matter—the art of bodybuilding. The next six to nine months also consisted of proper dieting, rest, discipline, and sacrifices. I met Paul three days a week for two hours a day. Our routine consisted of mid-to-deep leg squats of about 150 to 200 pounds, bench presses, and power cleans of about 175 to 200 pounds. We did a twenty-minute cooldown period for arms and legs only after each workout session.

My initial body weight was 160 pounds. My physique transformed into something special after all was said and done. I was 175 pounds and started to feel a whole lot better about myself. My mother's earlier comments never came up again. Please allow me to thank my Lord and savior for putting Brother Paul in my path at a time of weakness and despair. He didn't know what vital role he played in my success in achieving my ultimate goal.

A Close Encounter with Joe Nettles, Jr.

Moment on the Football Field

I hadn't seen Joe in at least a decade. I ran into Joe while leaving the library. I had been writing intensely. I was headed to my car when I noticed a man and woman along my path. Just as I moved over a tad bit, I caught a glimpse. Just to be sure, I went ahead and asked, "Are you Joe Nettles?" He responded, "Yes, I am."

I followed up by asking, "Do you know who I am?" He paused for about ten seconds before calling me by my first name. I replied, "Yes, it's me, brother. How have you been?"

He went on to say, "Oh, I'm well."

I shared with him some jaw-dropping news concerning my book. I went on to tell him that I was working on my memoir with hopes of having it ready for publication soon. He wished me the best on my memoirs, and then, out of nowhere, hit me with a short story about our time at Istrouma Junior High School, some forty-six years ago. I was fifteen years old at the time. Initially, I wasn`t sure why he wanted to share this story with me after so much time had passed. Maybe that was a clever way to get me to write his story in, which worked by the way.

According to Joe, we lined up across from each other, down in a four-point stance on the football field. On the sound of Coach G's whistle, we attacked each other with the intended purpose of putting the other on the ground. Joe went on to say that I hit him so hard that he literally saw stars. He knew football wasn't for him after that field encounter.

Joe, I'm so sorry. Never knew this before now. Wow! What a gracious guy to allow me the privilege of sharing his story with you. In closing, Joe was quite a basketball player in his own right. He later developed a love for the sport of boxing.

This Week in Pro Football

In the early '70s, there was a show that aired on weekends called *This Week in Pro Football* hosted by Tom Brookhier and Pat Summerall. These men were insightful in the game of football. I thought it was fun to watch week in and week out. The show was centered on games that were played the week before with plenty of excerpts and music. It had a lot to offer to the audience such as watching those great professional athletes in action, making long runs for touchdowns, and catching long touchdown passes. I often pondered how nice it would be to play the game of football in front of millions of people. I know. Wake up. But that was how I thought as a 15-year-old kid.

Little did I know; my dreams would actually come true.

My Water Baptism: for the Remission for My Sins

Before I get to the next iconic story in my life, let's go back several years earlier. I was ten years old. My mother wanted all of her children to experience water baptism at an early age. God answered her prayers. My big brother, Saymon Jr., and my big sister, Gertie, had their experience several years prior. I would pick their brain about it from time to time; both of their stories were similar. For example, from their point of view, it was like a crossover to another dimension with a quick burst of light to guide your faith to something tremendously special. That was really a wow moment for me just to know.

My mother always found time to talk to us about the water baptism and what it represented in our lives. The baptism is a symbol of Christ's burial and resurrection and a requirement to get into heaven. This was based on our faith and belief, which were instilled in us at a very young age.

Finally, the day came for my water baptism. All the talking and brain-picking was done. Of course, I was a little scared and nervous at first. I was just a ten-year-old kid. The mere idea of being submerged in a pool of water was a little intimidating for me. Nevertheless, there was no turning back; it was time to take a dip in the name of the Father, Son, and Holy Ghost. I felt renewed when I came out of the water. It was just like my big brother and sister described it to me.

My church family and immediate family were so proud of me that day. My biggest cheerleader was my mother. The moment she prayed for had finally arrived. I was the third of five siblings to experience the water baptism. However, I waited another six years to experience the dream the encounter of a lifetime: My born again experience.

My Born Again Transformation: He Gave Me Eternal Life

Here's another significant moment. There was no way I could have predicted what was coming next.

One weekday afternoon in 1973, my friends, Glen Grisby, Ronald Washington, and I were just hanging out shooting the breeze. Suddenly the idea of playing a pickup game of basketball came up. We all agreed, found a basketball, and proceeded to what was then Fairfield Park. It wasn't long into our journey before we encountered our neighbors David and Ruby. They appeared out of nowhere and asked, "Hey, where are you guys off to?" We responded, "Fairfield Park for a few rounds of basketball."

They informed us they were having Bible study and asked if we would like to come sit in for a while. Me my friends Glen and Ronald, looked at each other and momentarily hesitated before we accepted their invitation to join them. We figured a moment of Bible study wouldn't take very long. Next thing I knew, we were led inside by David and Ruby. There were other people present that day. We all began a study in the Word after a brief introduction.

As time passed, questions were raised such as "why is faith so important in our lives?" and what are "wages of sin? By now, my boys and I were wondering what's next since it was getting late. Group prayer followed. We were all asked to find a place in the room to kneel down and worship the Almighty God! At this point, Glen, Ronald, and me were a part.

We wanted the study to end. Then David and Ruby said, "Listen, just repeat these three words after us, 'Thank you, Jesus.' over, and over again." I didn't think much about it at first. Why? Many years prior to this encounter, my mom, a devoted Christian woman, introduced

my siblings and me to the Lord, God, His Holy Word way back in our youth. However, I had no idea what was coming next for me.
So about two to three minutes into calling on the name of Jesus, it happened. Still on my knees in prayer, it felt like an angel ascended upon me from above, and just like that, I found myself swaying from side to side and praising God with my hands raised for joy. Finally, after I came out of the zone of praise I was in. David and Ruby were standing by waiting to congratulate me. My first question to them was, "Can you tell me what just happened?"

They said, "Brother Charles, your day of salvation has come and you are born again, for the angels in heaven are rejoicing before God." I was stunned. The only word I could think of at that time was "wow"! while standing there with my eyes yet full of tears.

Out of concern for my friends, I asked where Glen and Ronald were. David and Ruby told me that they got up and left after group prayer. For a moment, I felt like my two friends had abandoned me. Seeing how we came together, one would think we would leave together. However, it was not the case on that day.

David and Ruby escorted me home and explained what happened to my mom after things settled down. I stood there alongside David and Ruby as they explained. Believe me when I say my mom knew there was something different about her son in a positive way. She saw it first hand and up close. After they finished with all the details concerning my encounter, out of nowhere, they popped the question and asked Mom if I could join them for a midweek church service. First Mom asked if I wanted to go. I replied yes. So, off to church we went. My mother gave David and Ruby her permission and told them what time they needed to have me back home no matter what.

My mom continued shaping and cultivating my spiritual values in the following months and years. She taught me, along the way, one of my biggest tests yet to unfold concerning my father. It did not manifest itself until the Fall of '79. However, this was one of those pivotal moments in my life that would last an eternity.

Before closing this story, I would like to thank David and Ruby for playing such a vital role in my life that weekday afternoon in 1973. May God's blessings rain down on you and your family forever.

Therefore, if any man be in Christ, he is a New creature: old things are passed away; behold all things become new. (II Corinthians 5:17)

A Call to Enroll in Capitol High School

I was sixteen years old; it was time to enroll in high school and study there for the next three years. That meant many things for me. I was ready to experience a new school, new teachers, new friends, and new coaches. I knew there would be many more good things to look forward to such as proms and graduation.

It wasn't long before flyers were posted for football tryouts. Long story short, I tried out and made the JV- squad with ease. My new position was Defensive End, and I was a pretty good one at that. There were some at my new school who found me to be a little cocky, conceited, and even a little self-centered. However, I found the thought process they had of me to be nothing more than perception, not reality. Because I knew the words spoken about me were not true.

The flyers for Junior Varsity basketball tryouts were posted after football season concluded. Of course, I was one of many to sign up for an opportunity to earn a position on the squad. I made the cut by the skin of my teeth. However, that feeling of jubilation did not last. A week or so later, prior to the first basketball game, I began experiencing severe stomach pain. The pain was so intense that I thought it was a virus of some sort. Nope. My mother and father found out it was something much more serious than that—it was Appendicitis.

I was rushed to the hospital for an emergency medical procedure, which was a success in Jesus' name. I can't thank God enough for sparing my life through it all. I will always be grateful for his mercy. I guess you can imagine how that incident shook my family and me up pretty good. I hoped I had a chance to rejoin my teammates after my recovery, but it was too late. My position had been filled. My coach didn't know how much time I needed to recover from surgery.

Nevertheless, my mother felt I needed to take time away from sports to heal and focus on my studies. So that's what I did. I didn't have much of a choice in the matter.

I learned that no matter how hard you work at certain things in life, they're just not meant to be. Case in point: basketball.

The Shelby Jackson Football Field Encounter

I was a sixteen-year-old. It was my sophomore in high school. I tried out for the football team and made it as a Defensive End. I wasn't a very big lad at the time. I stood about five feet ten inches tall and weighed about 175 pounds. I was pretty tough on the football field before I met this fellow by the name Shelby Jackson. I had no idea who he was, but I soon found out. We were on the field going through a warm-up session prior to practice. Shortly thereafter, we were put into individual groups by position.

So, it happened Me and Shelby were in the same group. That matchup with Shelby Jackson defined my football career forever. Shelby weighed 235 pounds and stood about six feet one inch in height. He was strong as an ox and tough with a nasty disposition on the football field. This is how our encounter played out: We were going through a series of contact drills when, all of a sudden, I came across-yep! Shelby. At first glance, I didn't think much of him. However, over the next fifteen minutes or so, my thought process about him changed.

The first time we lined up across from each other it was in a four-point stance, was I intimidated? Of course not. At the sound of

Coach Doe's whistle, we attacked one another with the intended purpose of winning. Shelby fired out with such an intense hit that I was shook me so badly that I wanted to walk away and quit the game I loved forever. But there was something instilled in me at an early age that wouldn't allow me to quit. It was called intestinal fortitude.

Round two was about to begin. This time I was ready, at least that's what I thought. Again, down and set, and we attacked each other again at the sound of the whistle. I was able to get a little bit of an edge by staying low and driving hard all the way through. However, that good feeling was short-lived. Round three was the last time I faced Shelby on the football field in that capacity. There we were again, lined up across from one another. At the sound of the whistle, we were back at it. This time I attacked him with everything I had left in me but to no benefit because in the end, he flattened me like a pancake.

Truth be told, I wasn't much of a match for Shelby. That day was like facing someone with a breastplate of armor. He made me realize I would most likely want to consider a position change if I was to continue playing the game. The following year, I did.

Thank you, Shelby Jackson, for helping me make a smart decision concerning my football career.

New Position Change Try Out

I remember a teammate from Istrouma Jr. High. His name was Len Willet. He was a pretty good athlete. Some three years later we reacquainted ourselves on the football field at Capitol High School. This time under different circumstances: He was trying out for a Wide receiver position, and thanks to Shelby Jackson I was also trying out for a new position.

During the ono-on-one drills, Defensive Back versus Wide Receivers, my old teammate Len Willet lined up across from me, came off the line, and drove me back for an instant! I recovered quickly after he broke off his route to slant. To make the catch I hit him with so much force he coughed it up, and never returned to the game of football again.

All that I could say to that was "wow, sorry, bro!" This is new insight… Just thought you, the reader, would like to know.

Paul Martin, Creator of Teammates' Nicknames

According to *Wikipedia*, a "nickname" is a "substitute for the proper name of a familiar person, place, or thing, for affection or ridicule."

Here's a lite profile on my friend and teammate Paul Martin. He stood about six feet one inch, weighed about 175 pounds. He had good speed, he was smart with good ball-catching skills, and last but not least, he was a crafty receiver.

I never knew why Paul took it upon himself to create these Historic nicknames, but he did. Here are a few nicknames to share for the ages over: Elgin "Who" Stewart, Richard "Yo-Yo" Williams, Doug "Undertaker" Morgan, Bobby "The Juice" White, Ralph "Rig" Griffin, Michael "Hot Foot" Davis, Wilbert "Crazy Legs" Jordan, and last but not least, Charles "Outlaw" Jefferson.

Again, thanks, Paul, for the time and research you put into generating those nicknames. Well done.

The Steve Angrum Effect

There were weaknesses about my game that needed strengthening going into my junior year. Who better to call on than an old friend of mine, Steve? We reacquainted one summer afternoon at Fairfield Park. Steve was six feet one inch, weighed 230 pounds, was hardworking, smart, and a beast on the football field. I mentioned my concerns to Steve and how I needed some help to improve.

I wanted to build more muscle mass, body weight, strength, and power. After a few days, Steve agreed to help me attain the goals I had set for myself that summer. I only had three months to get it done. I believed Steve was the one who could take me to the next level to increase my strength and keep me focused along the way. The first month of training included a series of grueling weight exercises.

It was the moment of truth for me to prove to him how badly I wanted to succeed. He pushed me extremely hard during our work out sessions which was something I desperately needed. I had invested too much in this to walk away. I knew my limitations and did not plan to exceed them. He also suggested a diet change which would incorporate eating more foods that were high in protein such as steak, chicken, and fish. He introduced additional proteins as what he called a "milk-and-egg shake" with a hint of vanilla extract. I would mix it, shake it, and drink it three times a day for two to three months with a garden salad as a side dish. I Followed his road map to the end. The results were great. Steve was one of the nicest individuals I had the pleasure and opportunity of working with on my way to the Nation Football League.

As I close out this tale, I would like to personally thank Brother Steve for his time, wisdom, and mentorship when I needed it the most. Lastly, thanks for being a friend who played a vital role fulfilling my dream.

When It Comes to Football Tips from My High School Mentors

Michael Bryant and Gregory Terrance were my high school mentors. Michael stood about six feet one inch tall, weighed about 185 pounds. He was fast, agile, tough, smart, and a hard-hitter when he had to be. He also possessed great one-on-one cover skills and a threat on the offensive side of the ball as well. Rumors had it, he once threw a football over eighty yards while on the move. He was a terrific athlete. As a junior in a backup role to these guys, all I could do was learn, watch, and wait. I did that with a great deal of patience.

Gregory Terrance was my other mentor. He stood about six feet tall and weighed about 190 pounds. He also had good one-on-one cover skills, which came with a nasty disposition on the field. He was somewhat hot-headed off the field. In other words, he was an intimidator. Everyone on campus knew it. Again, I learned from those guys for one year. That's all it took. They both stayed on my case. I'm sure they had good intentions for me. It just took me awhile to figure out that they saw something special in me.

They knew my talent level and were not going to let up on me until it manifested. It was a tad intimidating at first. However, like so many other things in the past, I got through it. I took everything my two mentors taught me about the game of football and incorporated it into my game in the years to come.

Because of Michael, I became one of the best shutdown corners to ever play the game. Because of Gregory, I learned to play the game as an intimidator and killer on the field.

Thanks, Michael and Gregory, for believing in me through it all.

Jerome Sellars, A Good Friendship Story

I met Jerome in the Fall of 1974 through my big brother, Saymon Jr. It didn't take long for us to size each other up and realize we had quite a few things in common such as a winning spirit, girls, money, and the rewards of hard work. He weighed about 175 pounds, stood about five feet ten inches tall, had brown eyes, brown hair, was street-smart. He also had a great deal of common sense to offer. He was just the type of person I needed to form a relationship with.

In the following months, Jerome and I became more than good friends—we became brothers at heart for a lifetime. He was someone I could trust and talk to about anything under the sun. We were just that close. I loved him like my own kid brother. I remember talking to him one afternoon about my dream of playing football on Sunday in the National Football League (NFL). He just laughed at first. He later said, "What can I do to help you attain this dream?" The first thing I did was appoint him as my speed and conditioning coach to help me attain my goals of someday playing in the NFL. His job on any given day was to work me to the brink of giving up. And believe me, he knew how to do it when it counted the most.

I'll explain more about this later. For the next three years, Jerome helped me put together one of the most grueling workout regimens of its time. Those drills were hard. They were meant to make you or break you. Let me share a few of them:

1. Forward and backward hill climbing: It was perfect for acceleration development and a proper running technique. It was also a technique to strengthen your body to stay in proper form while performing on the field play.
2. Stadium stair climbing: This technique was a great way to build leg explosion, develop great cardiovascular endurance, and to tone your calf muscles and buttocks.
3. Ninety-degree stadium stair climbing: This method was great for horizontal movement such as agility and eye coordination.
4. Rope-skipping: I could skip-rope both forward and backward. It was a great technique for quickness and foot speed.
5. Swimming pool drills: This was a very creative technique. I was an excellent swimmer during my day. Meaning I could do it all— freestyle, backstroke, breaststroke, and swim under water equally as well. Pretty impressive, wouldn't you say?

The forward stadium stair climb was done three days a week in three repetitions of five. Most days we had to gain access to the stadium field before we could start. Afterward, we performed a warm-up session that consisted of stretching and calisthenics. Next, we walked over to the ground level of the stadium steps together. Jerome would line up adjacent to instruct me. I would then take position on the first step on the sound of his command, "On your mark, go." I would explode up the steps one at a time with extreme power, speed, and determination while gaining altitude to my destination, the topside of the stadium. At that point, I always paused a moment to catch a breath of fresh air before descending the steps slowly and carefully. By the time I touched down on the last step, I would quickly turn left or right on a 180-degree angle and explode back up with the same vigor and determination. I would do three repetitions of five sets three times a week for a total of two months.

The St. Augustine Scrimmage Game

It was our first scrimmage of the season. We were playing against St. Augustine High. They were well reputed from previous years and led by the Hall of Fame coach, Otis Washington. They were an aggressive, disciplined, and organized team. We were just as tough and well-coached as they were. We were under the leadership of Hall of Fame Coach Roman Bates, Jr. Neither team could make much offensive progress that afternoon. Somehow it seemed that a battle between the defenses was shaping up, which both were prolific. Four seniors led the team (Charles Jefferson, Ralph Griffin, Doug Morgan, and Shelby Jackson). Coach Bates challenged me as a senior in that game. He told me that I was to intercept three passes and return them all for scores. I had something to strive for even more.

The final statistics were: Several pass deflections, three pass interceptions returned for touchdowns, several bone-chilling tackles. I know it was just a scrimmage, but it felt good to beat those guys. I thought about all I had done after the game and how much I had improved since last season. I realized that all my hard work from the summer training paid off. I was ready to display my talent for everyone to see. I was still confident because of my performance in the scrimmage game. So, I was ready to showcase my talents once more. We were to play our jamboree game at Memorial Stadium against Broadmoor High. Many anticipated a large crowd to attend the game.

I was focused and ready to play. Just before the game, I peered out over the stadium and recalled all the hard work I put in several months earlier. As the game began, we took an early lead on Broadmoor. We dominated the game on offense and defense. I had a memorable night as Broadmoor was down the final five minutes of the game. Broadmoor was looking to score their first touchdown of the night. I lined up at the left side corner position. The play call came to my side of the field. My first reaction was to defend the pass first. Once I realized it was a run play, I had to readjust and come up to help with run support. It was an option play. The quarterback pitched the ball to the running back. The running back fumbled the ball. I went to pick it up but, I was hit on my right ankle. I fell to the ground in severe pain. I tried to move my foot, but it was unresponsive. I then realized that it was a good chance my ankle was broken. My teammate James, B. picked up the ball and ran it back for a seventy-five-yard touchdown. After a year filled with promise, one play ended my season just like that. And that was the last time I would wear the red and gold for the Capitol Lions on the football field.

I later learned that we would have possibly gone to the state championship had I not endured that injury. With the season behind me, I wasn't sure if I had done enough to earn a football scholarship. However, offers came from schools all over America for the like of Elgin Stewart, Ralph Griffin, Douglas Morgan, Richard Williams, and others. I was still waiting to hear from other schools. I was also thinking of joining the United States Marine Corp. or selecting a university to walk on so that I could earn a football scholarship to further my education. I believed that I still had a lot left to give to the game with my God-given talent. All I needed was a chance to prove it!

Meanwhile, many of my teammates were receiving and signing letters of commitment to universities to further their careers. I remained hopeful and confident. I knew my opportunity would come. Coach Bates kept me informed every week about schools that were looking for athletes. Then one day, it happened. Coach Bates called me to his office to tell me that a university in Lake Charles (McNeese State) had expressed interest in offering me a scholarship. I was excited about the news! Coach Bates had scheduled to meet with Moe O'Brien-- the scout and coach of McNeese.

One Sunday afternoon at Capitol High, the coaches met for three hours talking about my collegiate future with McNeese. McNeese wanted to see me in action on film from past games. Coach Bates only had two games of me on film from my senior year because of my injury. He also spoke personally about me to the coach. Coach shared how great a student I was, my character off the field, and that I was more than what they were looking for if given the opportunity. Coach shared that I was a heck of a player, and he believed I could definitely help improve someone's program.

My name was submitted to McNeese head football coach Jack Doland for further evaluation a week after Coach Bates met with the coaches.

While waiting to hear back from McNeese, another coach at Memphis State University, Coach Clark, mentioned me to McNeese. He noticed me while scouting for other players at Capitol High. They didn't have an open position for me, but he took notice that I was a good athlete. Thank you, Coach Clark, from Memphis University, for your keen eye for the talent within me.

In the end, I accepted the football scholarship offer from McNeese, who welcomed me with open arms. I want to thank my head coach, Coach Roman Bates, Jr., for believing in me. I always made sure to represent the red and gold—Capitol High Lions the right way.

Go Lions!

"Just Thought You Would Like to Know" Moments

There were many times I seriously considered giving up on writing my first book. One instance took place in the summer of 2016. I was diagnosed with a severe case of Arthritis and Tendinitis in my right thumb. Since I'm right-handed, it was sometimes a struggle for me to write and type my story. However, I made a vow to my family, friends, fans, and myself to finish my book.

I want to thank my Lord and Savior, Jesus, for providing me with everything I've asked of him and more. I will forever be grateful to him for all he has done for me. I hope to inspire at least one person by telling my story so that someone else will be brave enough to share theirs.

I did my absolute best to make it an interesting and enjoyable read for everyone. One of my favorite Bible Verses:
I can do all things through Christ which strengthen me.
-Philippians 4:13

Two Brothers' Last Showdown!

Hand-to-hand combat

I was just a kid trying to find my way and earn the respect of my big brother. I always looked up to him. He was one of my biggest admirers growing up. Although I never liked it when he put me in headlocks until I gave in, or how he always made me tap out when we wrestled. We shared many father-like moments. For example, when I was away from home, hanging out with neighborhood kids on the corner, for my protection, Big Brother would find me and say, "Get off the corner. You can play at home." I was always embarrassed to leave my friends that way.

Growing up with a Big Brother had its advantages and disadvantages. I did not know at that time that my mother was instructing him to keep an eye on me and to protect me. I probably would have had a better understanding regarding my upbringing had I known then what I know now. After all the tough love my big brother put me through growing up, I knew someday the time would come for me to stand up to him. I felt our last fight would play a key role in my future development as a young man.

I was seventeen years old. My physical status was different. I was five feet, eleven inches tall, and weighed about 185 pounds. My brother and I had our share of fights, as most brothers did. No matter how hard I fought back, I could never win, but I never stopped trying. After seventeen years of trying, something had changed. I later found myself in a rematch with my brother; this time, his winning streak was over. We fought and argued over money, position, personal items, and sometimes even out of jealousy.

Here is my version of what took place on one Fall afternoon in 1974: I completed my chores. So, I asked mom if I could go to Fairfield Park for a round of basketball with a couple of friends. She replied, "Sure, son. Don't be out late. You have homework." Just as I was about to exit the yard, guess who showed up! Big brother. It wasn't long after he greeted me at the front gate that there with bad news. He looked down at my shoes and noticed that I was wearing a pair of his athletic socks. He wanted me out of them immediately. However, he was all over me before I could respond to his request. The next thing I knew, the tussle was on over a pair of socks.

We exchanged several body blows. There were also a few headlock exchanges during the tussle. My mother witnessed it all. She didn't like it, not one bit-especially after she learned what triggered the fight. My mother screamed at the top of her lungs for him to stop it. Finally, he did. My brother busted my lower lip and made me bleed a little that day. Although that was the last fight with my brother, somehow, I felt we grew closer because of it. I also believed he knew I wasn't someone he could boss around anymore.

Something inside my head clicked after allowing things to settle down. I hated how I felt after that encounter with my brother over socks. Afterward, I vowed that I would not let anyone take anything away from me ever again. Big Brother had done his part in helping me prepare for life. At that point in my life, I was quite capable of handling my own matters. For the record, during my four years of college, not one time did I have to call on my big brother to defend my honor. Again, thank you, Big Brother, for your love, protection, and support through it all.

The Raymond Martin Storyline

Raymond and I were friends in junior high school, some 47 years ago. He was also a Baton Rouge native. We were football teammates as well as friends and classmates. I remember Big Ray, as we called him, as a soft-spoken, nice, gentle, and well-mannered individual. He had a mean streak on the football field. I witnessed many of his plays on the field, whether at practice or in an actual game. He played on offense and I played on the defense. I was able to watch him from the sideline showcasing his talent. Occasionally, I would make an appearance on the offensive side of the ball as a running back. It was nice to follow his lead. After a couple of years of playing football together in junior high, we moved onto different high schools. We reunited three years later by coincidence. McNeese State University offered both of us football scholarships.

We were all asked to stand one-by-one and identify ourselves by name and school at the first freshman football team meeting. After several introductions, a big, curly-haired, barrel-chested guy stood and said he was Raymond Martin from Baton Rouge. He said that he attended Central High School. I had a chance to talk to Raymond and explain who I was and how we knew each other after the introductions were done. I told him we attended Istrouma Jr. together several years earlier. Then he said yes, I know who you are. Charles Jefferson, right?"

I replied, "Yes, it's me."
He then replied, "You're a lot bigger since I last saw you."
"Likewise," I told him.

We had no idea of the impact we would make together over the next four years. Big Ray and I were teammates and brothers on the field and good friends off the field. In my humble opinion, Raymond was one of the best offensive linemen I had ever played with on the collegiate level. His credentials speak for themselves. I remember him, earning his first All-SLC Team, All-Louisiana Team, McNeese Football Hall of Fame, and SLC- 1970 All-Decade Football Team.

In Memory

I am grateful for the chance I had to share some of our experiences growing up- more importantly, concerning our football careers at Istrouma Junior High and McNeese State University. I pray that God continues to bless your family.

Sincerely, Charles Ray Jefferson and Family

Rest in peace, my brother.

Four-Year Collegiate Career

Freshman Year

It was mid-August in the year 1975 in Lake Charles. I was at McNeese State University, preparing for school and my football career as one of the Cowboys for the next four years. It was time to get down to the business of school and football after the coaches and players made their formal introductions. We put in a couple of hard days of work on the field before it was time to share new nicknames. I did not expect nicknames to come up so early on in camp. I later learned nicknames became a popular part of who we were on and off the field at McNeese. These are just a few players I had the opportunity to play with during my freshman year: Bobby "Baby Bull" Wilson, "Bad Bob" Howell, Mitch "Tight" Tyson, Jim "Pous" Pousson, Anthony "Head" Nelson, Harry "Shank" Price, Mike "Super Mac" McArthur, and many others. As for me, a freshman defensive cornerback from Capitol High School, my nickname was Charles "Outlaw" Jefferson.

During my first training camp experience, I reported in superb physical shape to compete for a starting position on the squad. By the end of camp, I hadn't cracked the starting lineup yet. I was relegated to backup corner and special teamer during my first year. In the weeks and months to come, I finally settled into my role as a back-up corner and special teamer. As the season progressed, there were injuries on the defensive side of the ball at my position. It allowed me to play and showcase my skills on the field as a temporary starter. Although it was only for two weeks, the coaches liked the way I filled that role and felt that more opportunities present themselves for me.

Four weeks later, I experienced my first collegiate interception against Marshall University in Huntington, West Virginia. My coach told me to go in the game with about three minutes left to play. With time running out, Marshall tried me at my corner position. I went up high and over the intended receiver and intercepted the pass. My pass interception closed out the game. I had learned a great deal about the game, although I only had one year of college football experience. After an average season of play, at least that's what I thought, I noticed that players were bigger, faster, stronger, and in some cases, smarter. My position coach said, "before Charlie leaves, he is going to be in the top crops of cornerbacks that we've ever had, and I mean the class of Rocke Fournet, and Bryan Thompson." Coach Ernie said that all I needed was a little seasoning and I would be one of the best who ever played the game. He felt I had quick feet, quick reaction, toughness, great hands, and craved contact on the field. Enclosing: He said those traits made me a complete cornerback.

Sophomore Year

I took a world of knowledge and experience with me into my sophomore season in 1976. I realized if I wanted people to know who I was on the field, I had to work harder behind the scenes and earn their respect. No questions about it; I knew there were some areas of weakness in my game that needed attention. I worked hard over the summer for the next three months in hopes of improving and building on my strengths for the upcoming season. I strived for several things to help my performance on the field. My first focus was on weight loss. I ended the season at 185 pounds. I needed to lose ten pounds to regain quickness and straight-line speed. Secondly, I revisited my weightlifting regiment, which consisted of flat/vertical bench presses and a variation of push-ups- an old favorite of mine. The regiment included triceps push-ups, partner push-ups, forearm push-ups, clap push-ups, and the diamond push-ups. Those exercises helped develop the hand and forearm power that I needed.

I learned a technique for hand-strength and power years prior. Speaking of hand strength, here's an old tale concerning my father and a family friend. My father has always been an avid reader of newspapers. He reads the newspaper seven days a week with great passion. I know my love for reading comes from him. Depending on where you live, the average size of a newspaper ranges from 52-100 pages from Sunday to Saturday. One day, I was hanging out with one of my neighborhood friends who had large and extraordinarily powerful hands. He told me that he'd let me in on a little secret that had something to do with a newspaper if I wanted hands like his. He told me to take one page of the newspaper and put it in my dominant hand. Next, grab the corner edge and start rolling it slowly into a ball, toss it away, and grab another one. He instructed me to keep going until I couldn't anymore. I alternated hands on occasions. He was right after three months or so. A simple hand technique improved my hands' size and power. Thank you, Dad, for purchasing so many newspapers.

Preparing for what would be my best year ever on the collegiate level, I also looked to my little brother, who was a Coach for speed and conditioning, Jerome Sellers. Together we worked on improving my forty-yard dash times, back-peddling, foot speed, and some one-on-one play. We would always find time for hill-running and stadium climbing. To this day, I am forever thankful for Jerome Seller's time, support, and expertise that he would lend that summer. Having gone through an enormous amount of off-season work, I was ready to go back and compete. I looked forward to the first day of camp.

I did not waste any time my first day back during my sophomore year. We started with a team conditioning test for defensive cornerbacks and had to run a mile in six minutes. I was one of several players in my group who finished within six minutes among the defensive backs. I finished in five minutes and fifteen seconds. It was one of the fastest in camp. I reported to camp in super condition and was ready for my best year ever. I went from weighing 185 pounds to 175 pounds. I was ready to make my mark in history. I had finally earned a starting position at left cornerback after a long, grueling camp. Off-season training coupled with hard work in the camp had paid off for me.

We were playing against Southern Illinois University the opening day, and the score wasn't even close. We won with a score of 38 to 10. If I may say so, I played well that night as a starter and a special team player. However, I had not been tested on the corner as a defensive back until the second game of the season, which was to be against Louisiana Tech Bulldogs. I heard many stories about the mystique and legendary players on their past teams. Guys like Fred Dean, Roger Carr, Pat Tilley, Johnny Robinson, Terry Bradshaw, and many others were on the offensive side of the ball. The players were big, fast, and explosive. They had the skills to score from anywhere on the field at any time. Those guys were just that good. Our game plan was "execute, do your job, and then we win." That is how I remember the scouting report for the Bulldogs match up. The defensive scouts made it clear that we had to stop their wide receiver Billy Ryckman, quarterback Phil Robertson, and running back John Henry White in order for us to win.

We knew this was going to be a challenge; however, our coaches had a plan to stop their high-scoring machine. I did not know that I would play a vital role in our success at that time. Just as the scouting report was wrapping up, my position coach stood up, looked over to me, and said, "Charlie, you got Ryckman." Knowing there were other upperclassmen on the squad whom I felt could do the job, I asked "*Why me*?" I learned after the game that I was chosen to go against Ryckman to showcase my talent. Ryckman was an ALL – Southland Conference, All-American player who led the nation in past receptions. He averaged seven to eight catches per game.

He was like poetry in motion in film. He was smooth, fluid, and could run every route imaginable on the football field. Although he wasn't the fastest on the field, when it came to smarts, he was right up there with the best of them. I had always craved one-on-one matchups, whether it was on the football field, basketball court, running track, etc. So, this matchup was perfect for me to define my talent for the duration of my collegiate career. I practiced long and hard in preparation for my biggest test leading up to the game. It was clear that I wanted people to know who I was, and sure enough, after this game, they would.

During the big game that Saturday night in Bulldog Stadium, the time had come to put up or shut up with no excuses. My family, friends, teammates, and fans were all watching the game. Some were listening to the game on the radio. Others were watching it via television. As I stood on the sidelines alongside my teammates, my defensive coach came to me and said, "Just play hard and be who you are, Charlie." I found myself prancing around, filled with anticipation awaiting the start of the game.

The time had come for us to take the field on defense for the first time that night. I waited momentarily to locate Ryckman, just as we practiced all week after huddle break. Throughout the following sixty minutes, untested sophomore cornerback, Charles "Outlaw" Jefferson, went up against the nation's top receiver. Remember, he averaged seven to eight catches a game; however, my job was to shut him down that night. I did. He only managed one reception against me. I intercepted a pass made by Robertson that was intended for Ryckman at the 48th yard line.

The Rundown!

My speed and conditioning coach, Jerome Sellers, and I created something called "the rundown" during an off-season training session. I would line up in the middle of the field on the fifty-yard line with Coach Sellers at about the forty-yard line facing me. He wasn't a burner but, on a good day, he could run a 4.7-second forty-yard dash. He was fast enough for what I intended for him to do. I stood in the middle of the field, waiting for movement from Coach Sellers. Suddenly, he broke out in a sprint towards the end zone. It was then my job to "run him down" before he crossed the goal line. I did not realize that training regimen would come into play three months later, but it did.

Back to the game: I lined up across from Ryckman at the left cornerback. The dogs were moved back five yards after an offside penalty on their first snapback. Next, White swept around the left end behind a convoy of blockers where he broke off a tackle for twelve yards down the field. He then sprinted another 62 yards before I could get off my blocker and run him down on the 20-yard line from the backside of the field. All the hard work I put in had paid off. We closed out the game with a win that night.

Trust in the lord with all thine heart; and lean not unto Thine own
understanding. In all thy ways acknowledge him,
And he shall direct thy paths. -Proverbs 3:5,6

My Next Big Matchup

I've always loved one-on-one's. My next big one-on-one matchup didn't come until the fifth game of the season against the University of Louisiana at Monroe. It was another away game in front of a hostile crowd. I had the daunting task of shutting down another great receiver by the name of James Floyd. He stood about six feet, three inches tall, weighed about 185 pounds, and possessed world-class speed. James was feared by many for taking the top off of the defense. His intermediate route running was deemed average at best. I had a few more games under my belt by then, which meant more experience and confidence in my favor. We performed individual drills all that week with several of the fastest players on teams lined up against the cornerbacks and ran routes in preparation for the game. Several players ran 4.3 to 4.4 ranges in the forty-yard dash. This technique helped me wake my legs for fast running, and it worked. The defense was on the field for the first time, set, and ready to play. Just as expected, I was locked in on Floyd—this was my job the entire night.

That turned out to be one heck of a matchup for both of us. James was the first player to ever beat me deep in a real-time game. It happened that night. It came in the third or fourth quarter. I was lined up at left cornerback across from James. At the snap of the ball, James's purpose was to get deep in a hurry, even if it meant blowing past me. We ran down the sideline in an all-out foot race, going neck-to-neck for sixty yards. The ball was in the air. James was able to go over me and make the catch around the ten-yard line. Although he did not score on the play, it felt strange because I had never been beaten deep before. It was a close game, but we won that night. The end-game statistics finished with several tackles, one pass breakup, two pass deflections, and one interception. James had three catches that game.

Defensive Player of the Week Award

Our opponent was Eastern Michigan University at Cowboy Stadium. My endgame statistics were three solo tackles, one pass interception, three pass deflections, and I struck an end zone blow to shake loose a certain Huron touchdown pass that could have changed the outcome of the game. That was the first of many awards to come that year. I received the player of the week award for that game.

Independence Bowl:

We lost sixteen players throughout the season due to suspensions and eligibility rules. A local sportswriter referred us as a junior varsity squad. Although the players found the media comments demeaning, we would gain respect back later.

We finished the season strong by winning the Southland Conference and earned an invitation to play in the first Independence Bowl in Shreveport. We played against the Tulsa Golden Hurricanes. That was a game we wanted to win badly. We wanted to win the conference with a passion. We were ready to compete and win that night, thanks to the outstanding preparation by our coaching staff. My job was to cover their top receiver, Corn Webster. I shut him down the entire game. It was a close game, but we won with a score of 20 to 16. My endgame statistics included one interception, six solo tackles, two pass deflections, and one bone-jarring tackle on Corn Webster. We became the Southland Conference Champions as well as the Independence Bowl champions.

However, it wasn't over for me; there was more good news to come. I was unanimously selected for the first team All-Southland Conference the same year. I led the team with eight interceptions and forty-one solo tackles. I was also selected for the All-Louisiana Collegiate Football team. Overall, that was one special year—a year I will never forget.

There was a movie released in December of that year entitled *A Star is Born* starring Barbra Streisand and Kris Kristofferson. The movie turned out to be quite a masterpiece. Although I hadn't seen it, my little sister Belvin apparently saw it and felt that I had shown enough on the football field to be worthy of such an honor myself. So, my little sister presented me with something charming that she took the time to make. I held it up and read it. I stopped and teared up for a moment. Anyway, the four words I will always remember about that day were "A Star Is Born."

My Junior Year Campaign

I reported to camp in superb condition and with high hopes and expectations of winning another championship. I learned that I was selected as a candidate for the College Football All-America Team after a few days into camp. The good news fueled my expectations for the upcoming season. Several months earlier, during Spring camp, Coach Ernie said, "As a group, we had one of the best Spring workouts ever." He believed that the secondary was the strong point of the Cowboys. He also went on to say, "I can't believe my luck. I have all-starting players back for two more years. They are being led by All-America Team candidate, Charlie Jefferson."

That was my junior year. All I could think about was winning. We knew it was going to be a tough year for us on the field. Teams were looking to take our spot as champions. I was a target based on my reputation. The incoming freshmen felt they had to prove their worth during Fall camp. They wanted to compete against the best defensive back on the team. They quickly learned that I had a reputation for a reason. They eventually got the message that going against me in one-on-one matchups wasn't good for their health.

The season came and went. I had another outstanding year under my belt. I ended the season with four interceptions and forty-five solo tackles. However, we did not win the championship, nor did we get an invitation to another bowl game; I did not make the All-America Team. I earned a spot on the All-Southland Conference Team. I still had another year of eligibility left to accomplish some of those personal goals I set for myself.

My Senior Year Campaign

It was my last year. I was about to close out my collegiate football career at McNeese. I reported to Fall camp in pristine condition like many times before. My head coach, Jake Doland, had only had one losing season in his eight-year career at McNeese. After that one disappointing season, Coach was ready to get back to his winning ways. We had thirteen returning starters, thirty-four lettermen, and sixteen players who ran a 4.6-second forty-yard dash or better. According to Coach, speed and quickness indicated what they could expect from Senior Charlie Jefferson. He replied, "Charlie is a super athlete this season, and we expect him to play like one. The pro scouts are predicting he will go within the first three rounds of the draft."

I was considered one of the best cornerbacks in the south. We managed to improve our record to 7–4, which was better than the prior year. We played hard week in and week out. We badly wanted to bring a championship back to McNeese in hopes of returning to a bowl game. I guess it wasn't meant to be. We tried like hell, though. I was a starter for three years and led the team in interceptions. I was selected to the All-Southland Conference team for the third time. I was named as an Honorable Mention to the Associated Press (AP) All-American Team. I finished with 20 career interceptions and tied for eighth place on the All-time Louisiana players list.

Preparing for My Pro-Day Experience

Since my collegiate football career had come to an end, I needed to take time off to focus on my studies and heal up before starting the next chapter in my life. I knew I was going to be a professional football player based on legitimate sources. I was told I could be drafted as high as the first two rounds.

First, I needed a well-known and competent agent to represent me. By definition: A sports agent is a person who gets between 7 percent and 10 percent of the athlete's pay contract. They can also receive up to 10 percent to 20 percent of the athlete's endorsement contracts. Their primary job is obtaining the most money as possible from any team that's vying for your services. They also manage and guide you in making intelligent decisions throughout your career. There were so many distractions by phone, mail, and dorm visits. I had to find an agent quickly so that I could settle down and concentrate on my future.

I felt like a celebrity on campus for the first time in my life. I called Coach Hayes and asked for his guidance and expertise in the areas of speed and conditioning as Pro day was quickly approaching. Coach Hayes believed I had many of the intangibles that I needed to become a great professional athlete if I stayed injury-free. I found the one man who could help me achieve that goal. A few months before Pro day, my big brother informed me that the forty-yard dash is the defining moment of the whole event. Coach Hayes was the first person to explain to me, in detail, the technique of running the forty-yard dash correctly.

You should keep yourself at a forty-five-degree angle then slowly come up to a full running stance for the first ten yards. You should also pump your arms as fast as you can at a ninety-degree angle. Once your body is in the full running position, run through the finish line as fast as you can. I practiced the technique with the help of Coach Hayes' assistance for the next two weeks as needed. I was able to research and find some information from my sophomore football season. I ran a 4.6-second forty-yard dash that season. I was a senior. I was bigger, stronger, faster, and smarter. I also needed help with additional expertise in the field of running and pass-catching. I called three friends/classmates and a superstar track coach who all played a vital role in my success leading up to my first pro day. First, I called on my friend Harry Price. We weren't just teammates; we were roommates on campus as well. I then called another friend and teammate, Richard Ellender, who was well-liked and respected on campus. He was a wide receiver and punt-runner who aspired to play professional football. I asked him to train with me on route running on the field. I also called my friend Verril Young, an alumnus of McNeese. He was a track star. He helped me with my speed conditioning and technique.

I stayed in the weight room to maintain my strength during the training period and between football and track workouts. I got my forty-yard dash time down to 4.5–4.55 seconds on the track after weeks of training. Last but not least, I also timed at 4.58–4.6 seconds on the grass. Finally, it was time for my first test to determine how fast I could back-paddle over a ten-yard split. I had one of the fastest times ever recorded by a cornerback. The next test was the standing vertical jump. I was only given two attempts, and I had to wear football cleats. I cleared 33 inches on my first attempt. I cleared 36 inches on the final attempt. The next event was the forty-yard dash. It was the moment I had been waiting for. I clocked 4.53 seconds on my first attempt. I clocked 4.56 seconds on the second one. I felt pretty good about my results that day.

Pro day events were a week away. I had time to rest, relax, and study. Now that the numbers were in, a professional football weekly scouting magazine noted, "If Jefferson's times hold true in the forty-yard dash, he may be the second cornerback drafted." Another magazine would read, "Charles Jefferson is quick, tough, and agile. A smart and splendid Athlete. He excels against the pass and comes up tough to defend the run. He has good catch-up speed. And like other small college performers, he still has some proving to do, even though many scouts are convinced that he has the physical and mental requisites of a professional cornerback. The thoughts were that he should be the second or third corner to go off the draft board."

I was now ready for my second round of Pro day to start. This time,

several new scouts came for the show with a few different tests than before. The first drill was a quickness and agility test.
They strategically placed several orange cones across the field. I had to run around the cones and move at different angles as quickly as possible when told to do so. Afterward, the coaches told me that they were impressed by my agility skills. The second test was to assess my ball skills. They wanted to see how quick and strong my hands were (hand-catching drill) to determine my ball -catching skills. The third and final test of the day was the one-on-one matchups against wide receivers and tight ends. I was not intimidated at all. As a matter of fact, I was looking forward to it. I only allowed two caught passes out of twelve that day. As long as the scouts were impressed, that's all that mattered. I still had a series of interviews left at the end of the day. I was later told that the interview process went well. The second day was over, and it was time to relax and rest before the third and final pro day.

I thought it was time to stop and find an agent with draft day quickly approaching. So, I asked my teammate Richard if he knew of someone I might want to talk with. He recommended a guy that was a prominent realtor, Mr. Palermo. I asked Richard, "What does he know about the football business?" He told me to trust him and don't forget to tell him that he sent me. I called Mr. Palermo to schedule a meeting with him later that day.

I found that Mr. Palermo was a smart, hardworking, successful, businessman during my first meeting with him. I felt that he had my best interest at heart concerning my career. I had good feelings about it felt that he could be the agent for me. Before I committed, I had already scheduled to meet with another agent. However, it did not go over too well. We mutually agreed to move on. So, I met with Mr. Palermo once more, and I decided to sign him as my agent.

The third and final pro day consisted of agility drills, weight lifting, classroom interviews, and more coverage drills. I'm proud to say that I excelled in all of the events that day. A few days later, scouts said, "He's smart, craves physical contact, and can also be a prospect on the inside. Good Blitzer, mobile, and does well in passing situations." Once again, I was one of the top-discussed cornerbacks predicted to go in the professional football draft that year.

Timeline Leading Up to My Father's Horrific Accident

Just like any other Spring morning in April, my father would often leave earlier for work leaving behind a wife, son, three daughters, and a grand-daughter. After having put in a full day's work of ten-hours on the job, it was now time for dad to return home to his family. However, for some reason or another, he decided to stop by brother Willie Lee's home for a short visit. He continued home upon the conclusions of his visit. He had no idea what was coming next about ten minutes or so into his drive home on Greenwell Spring Road. Before turning left onto Lanier Drive, he stopped to yield for two passing vehicles with their lights on for safety that late afternoon. As he proceeded to turn onto Lanier, a third car without headlights would hit his car on the passenger door with such force that the impact would put him out cold. He said the last thing he remembered was waking up in the hospital three days later with bandages all over his body, fighting for his life in intensive care.

A Father's Horrific Auto Accident

Prior to the NFL Draft, my father was involved in an accident that had almost cost him his life. It was a tear-jerking encounter. I found it hard to believe at first, but when I received the call from my mother, she confirmed that it was true. I was back at school in Lake Charles at the time of the accident. My mother called and asked if I could come home to be with my father. She stated my father had a slim chance of surviving, according to the doctors. They believed that he might make it if he could get through the first 72 hours of his fight. She also shared that the doctors said that he would be confined to a wheelchair for the rest of his life if he survived-- having no chance to ever walk, run, work, or drive again. Knowing that my father had to fight for his life for the next 72 hours, I immediately got up and notified my agent and Coach Doland. I packed my bag to head home and be with my family. I drove back some two hours alone even though a friend asked to accompany me. I recall telling her, "I think it may be best if I go alone this time."

I had no idea what I was in for over the next two to three hours driving home. It took about two hours and fifteen minutes to drive home under normal circumstances, but the circumstances surrounding my father's accident felt more like three hours that day. I made several stops on my way back home.

First, at the age of twenty-one, the mere thought of losing my dad this way was unconscionable for me. I may have been wrong for feeling the way I did about my father, but he seemed to be invincible in so many ways. I remember asking myself, "How could this happen to such a good man? Why did it happen?" I know, who am I to question my creator? My drive home was filled with many emotional highs and lows. It was hard to manage the wheel and focus on the road with tears streaming down my cheeks. I was driven with love and passion to see my father. So, I pressed forward.

I finally made it home after a long and difficult drive. I was first greeted by my mother with a long, warm hug and kiss. I was then greeted by my siblings. My mother tried to prepare me as best as she could to see my father. When I walked through the door into the room and saw him, all that I could say was "Dad, I'm so sorry." I became overwhelmed by emotion. I fell to my knees and had to be escorted out of the room by my mother and a few others. It was hard to see my father in that light. My mother reminded me of a few things before I returned to school. She told me that Dad would get through with prayer, fasting, and love. She was right.

It's funny how things happen and bring about change overnight— like what happened to my dad. He was strong and willing to fight on for his family. The roles had switched. The family would have to become the caretakers and providers for Dad. We all had vital roles to play throughout our father's fight back to full recovery.

My father had to undergo intense rehabilitation programs at the hospital for the next three months. It would either make or break his will to live. He worked tirelessly on his comeback—sometimes even three times a day. If I had to choose one word to best describe my father during his recovery, it would be "perseverance" meaning—the quality that allows someone to continue trying to do something even though it is difficult. That was my father at his best.

It wasn't long before the doctors decided to move him to another facility in Houston, Texas to resume his rehabilitation. This time he had to go through the program alone. It was hard on all of us at first. Growing up, I don't ever remember my father being away from us for any substantial amount of time. Twice a day, five days a week, he fought with more determination than ever to prove he could get back to being the man he was before the accident occurred.

My dad made substantial improvements in his life over the next several years. It seemed that he was driven to prove to those who doubted him along the way. He also wanted to show people he could do the things the doctors said he would never be able to do anymore—walk, run, work, or drive. He proved to us all that it was possible to do all of those again through lots of hard work and prayer.

Some ten years later, I was fortunate enough to be led by the spirit of God to go to my father and pray with him the Sinner's Prayer one afternoon. My father accepted Jesus as his Lord and Savior.

It's been thirty-nine years or so since that accident happened. He has since retired from his last job of twenty-one years. My father is now ninety-three years old. He still wakes up early for his morning newspaper and coffee. He still enjoys his morning and afternoon strolls through the neighborhood when he can. And most importantly, he's still an awesome dad and man of God to be around. God isn't done with him just yet!

My 1979 Draft Day Experience

Draft day had come. My football agent Joe Palermo Jr. offered me an invitation to come and settle in with him and his family. I accepted the offer. Later he mentioned to me that another client of his would also be joining us.

"I think you may know him," he said. I replied, "Is that so?"
He stated, "It's your teammate, Richard." I replied, "Okay, cool."
It could be a short wait for me, or on the other hand, it could have become a long and tedious ordeal. May 3, 1979, the first round of selections were in; no phone call came for me. The second round of selections happened, and again, still no phone calls. It felt like I would be drafted in that round based on my homework and the contingent of certain teams' needs for the third round. Approximately four hours had come and gone. Yet, I still did not get a phone call. I was beginning to feel a bit disappointed, but I hadn't lost faith. One of my best qualities is how confident I am in my beliefs and faith in my Creator. I knew, beyond a shadow of a doubt, that my name would be called soon. The fourth round was underway. Sure enough, about thirty minutes in, the phone rang. It was Red Miller, the head coach of the Denver Broncos, calling to say, "Hey Man! Congrats! You are a Denver Bronco."
I replied, "It's an honor. Thank you, Coach."
He asked, "Are you ready to go to work and help us win?" I replied, "Yes, sir, of course!"

I was officially a Denver Bronco, drafted two days before my twenty-second birthday. It was an amazing birthday gift. **Who'd a thunk it?**
I want to share with you what it truly felt like that day, waiting for nearly eight hours to hear my name called. It was like being stranded on a remote island with some basic amenities such as a flashlight, battery-powered radio, a chair, sunglasses, canteen full of water, and the good book (the Bible)—having everything I needed, waiting for hours to be rescued. By sunset, all of a sudden, I received the phone call I had been faithfully waiting for.

Let me leave you with this: I was told that there are thirty-two teams in the National Football League, and it only takes one to be interested in your talent. It was the Broncos for me. I always wanted to be chosen

by a winning franchise like Denver, and I was. The truth be told, no sincere athlete will stand and say, "I really want to play for a losing franchise."
Before the draft in 1979, a Denver scout once shared with me that on draft day, they would like to draft a cornerback and shift Stephen Foley back to safety. I had no idea I would be the one in mind. I will never forget how this moment came about.

My Heavenly Father, who blessed me with an abundance of talent, placed me on a stage to showcase my talent.

In summary, I would like to thank my family, friends, coaches, and fans for their support throughout my journey.

Rookie Mini Camp Experience and My Seasons with The Houston Oilers

The Rookie camp was hosted for three days in Denver, Colorado. It was time to showcase my skills against other rookies and second-year players. I spent the next three days trying to validate the reason I was their fourth-round selection. Minicamp started with vigorous testing, team meetings, and special team meetings. There were field drills that consisted of seven-on-seven match-ups and one-on-one match-ups. The one-on-one match-ups were one of my favorites by far. I was able to come to a contract agreement with the Broncos while I was in Denver. It turned out well for everyone involved. I flew home to sort out some personal things and get down to business for my football career.

One day, while planning my off-season regiment, my agent Joe called me with some good news. He told me that I was chosen as "Outstanding Rookie" at minicamp. It was just what I needed to keep me motivated going into camp. However, nothing would be given to me at the next level in football. I would have to earn my way on the team. The Broncos' staff was there to help me achieve my goals.

They were kind enough to send me an off-season itinerary to help me prepare for opening day at training camp in Boulder, Colorado. My agent advised me about the differences in the climates between Denver and Louisiana. He told me to get into the best physical shape that I could. I asked him, "Why is that so important?" He said, "In case you didn't know, they don't call Denver the 'Mile High City' for nothing. It's officially 5,280 feet above sea level, which is equivalent to 1 mile, making it the highest major city in the United States. It makes the air there harder to breathe because of its altitude."

He also recommended that I book an early flight to Denver to get accustomed to the altitude. I reported to camp in the pinpoint shape- thanks to Joe. It wasn't long before I had to go through a conditioning test. For my group, the defensive backs had to run ten forty-yard dashes under six seconds with one-minute breaks. It was still a challenge for me due to the thin air and high altitude, although I considered myself to be in superb shape. I passed the conditioning test with flying colors. My focus returned to becoming the best cornerback there now that the conditioning session was behind me. It seemed promising during my first few days of camp.

One afternoon, while performing a dance routine shortly after dinner with other rookies, I made a sudden move to the right, and my leg unexpectedly shifted the wrong way. I hyperextended my right knee. I walked off the stage embarrassed. I could not believe what happened. It was odd that this setback could happen to me in camp. I had to report it to the medical staff to make things worse. They, in turn, told the coaching staff. For the next ten days, I had extensive rehabilitation on my right knee. I was ready to perform by the time the second pre-season game came. However, I had to clear the waiver wire to remain with the Broncos because of the NLF rules. While waiting to clear, The Houston Oilers, Atlanta Falcons, and New York Jets took notice of me. The Houston Oilers, now known as the Tennessee Titans, won me over. I had no say-so in the matter. Suddenly I was packing up and moving to Houston to join my soon-to-be new team. It was bittersweet to leave Denver. On the other hand, I was happy to be closer to home with family, friends, and fans.

I knew my role as a backup corner upon my arrival in Houston. Two established starters were already there. I had to wait for my opportunity to play. Meanwhile, I would enter the game on third downs as a Nickel-Back on some plays. I saw plenty of action on special teams too. It was cool to play with some of the greatest players who ever played the game. A few guys that come to mind are Earl Campbell, Elvin Bethea, Curley Culp, Robert Brazile Jr., Jack Tatum, Ken Stabler, Vernon Perry, and Carter Hartwig.

To summarize my first year with Houston: I played on special teams, and we made it to the playoffs. I had to re-establish my worth for the upcoming season. I performed and settled in well with my teammates throughout the training camp. My confidence returned to par after that strong finish at camp.

It was 1980, my second year with the Oilers' Franchise, and things looked promising. I was still a backup, but I was ready to step up whenever the opportunity presented itself. Throughout the season, I did play some secondary positions for injured players. Again, I spent most of my playing time on special teams. We made the playoffs again that year. We just flamed out at the end. It seemed as though there was about to be coaching staff changes to come.

It was time for me to step up big or get waived for the next season. Everyone was at risk. There were new coaches and some new players. I remember players called in by their position coaches and told what was expected of them that season. The players were dismissed if we did not meet the criteria laid out. My new head coach approached me about my talent one day. He said to me “Charles Jefferson, you’ve been blessed with an abundant amount of talent to play this game. I am counting on you to stay on the field. So, don’t get hurt or you may get cut too." Sure enough, minor injuries throughout camp eventually cost me my position going into my third season. I was asked to bring my playbook during the last and the final cut. At that moment, I knew that my services were no longer needed. Someone once told to me that the NFL stood for “Not For Long.” As far as I am concerned, those words still hold true today.

I had to call my parents and agent about the news. My agent asked me if I still wanted to play, but I wasn’t sure at that point. I told him that I needed time to think about it. My agent, Joe, mentioned the possibility of playing in the Canadian Football League for a while. Afterward, I could return and try my hand in the NFL again. It sounded like a good idea at first, but after playing in the NFL, I didn’t want to try another league. I decided to retire from football right then and there. I told him I was hanging up my cleats. I thanked him for everything he did during my NFL career. I remember something one of my coaches told me along the way: “You can’t play football forever. But, it’s a great way to get a financial head start in life- by doing something you love.”

Parting Shot Comments

Here are a few names of family and friends who were not written in this book but worthy of honorable mention:

Willie Lee Jefferson

Georgia Mae Jefferson

Joe Jefferson Jr.

Willie Mae Jefferson

Eric Jefferson

Faye Jefferson

Calvin Dillon

Mike Dillon

Bernard Bell

Reginald Brewer

Lionel Washington

Aaron Ward

Vernon Mills

Calvin Willis

David Stone

Blake Wellerman

Stanley Biemey

Sam Kemp

Levert Kemp

Robbie Collins

Gerald Gatlin

Roosevelt Price

Benson Magee

Lawrence Jefferson

Roland Briggs

Nathan Stewart, Sr.

Barry Carey

Larry Harris

Jerome Harris

Aldridge Allen

Joseph Calvin

Larry Clark

Dr. Jim Murphy

Louis Bonnette

Aston Jefferson

Michael Angrum

TRIBUTES

MOTHER AND FATHER ACKNOWLEDGMENT

There were five things mom and dad instilled in me during my youth: values, structure, personal discipline, focus, and dignity.

In terms of values, my parents taught me the difference between right and wrong, and consequences that come with decisions. They taught me the value of family and friends as well as the power of daily prayer in my life. In terms of structure, my parents taught me how to bridge things together the right way as I go through life. Learning personal discipline helped define the man I am today. In terms of focus, they helped me define my strengths and weaknesses as I went through many stages and milestones. My parents taught me the importance of dignity and to respect and honor those who are worthy of it. For example, if it's money, you have to go out and work for it. If its respect, you have and earn it.

A SON'S TRIBUTE

In honor of Breast Cancer Awareness Month:

1979 was a year of highs and lows for the Jefferson family. Of course, my father was still in a fight for his life due to the horrific automobile accident that occurred earlier in the year. Who knew that my mother would be diagnosed with Breast Cancer in her mid-forties later in the year? My mother instilled great Christian values in us that would last a lifetime. Once again, our faith, prayers, and trust in God was put to the test. For the next five-years, she too would be in a fight for her life, right alongside dad. My mother, throughout the horrible disease, was given an overwhelming amount of support and love during her fight with Breast Cancer from family, friends and a host of others. Consider this, for the next several years, my mother fought with every ounce of breath in her body to "win for us all," until the day she succumbed to the dreadful disease, Cancer. In closing, I would like to leave you all with one of my mother's favorite biblical verses to live by (believe me there were many but the one to best fit this storyline would be, Paul's last testimony):

> *"I have fought a good fight, I have finished my course, I have kept the faith: Henceforth there is laid up for me a crown of Righteousness, which the Lord, the Righteous Judge, shall give me at that day, and not to me only, but unto all them also that love his appearing."* II Timothy 4:7-8

Until we meet again.

Warm and sincere thoughts: Missing you so much!

Your son,

Charles Ray Jefferson

SUNSHINE: TRIBUTE TO MOM

Just the thought of our mother makes my days much brighter, my lonely days happier, and even my bad days are worth going through. She gave **so** much in such short time: five kids, a husband, sisters and brothers, and friends. Wow!

Your name *"Arcenia"* means powerful and complete!

What a treasure to have had you as a mother. You left each of us with your example, your smile, your grace, and your poise. Your desire to see your children succeed in life both naturally and spiritually will not be taken for granted.

MISSING YOU EVERYDAY!

I know that you are so proud of your baby son.

A FINAL TRIBUTE TO MOM

A Kind, Loving and Understanding Mother!

We could hear the faint flutter of your wings when you closed your eyes and soared to the Heavens for the final time. It was then we realized the master had called you home. It is hard not to week, for our lives grew out of your life. From the cradle, you along with father, nurtured, loved, labored, and sacrificed for us. When we needed you, you were there to give counsel in confused times, loving support in seasons of difficulty and praise in times of triumph. Nothing or no one can ever take your place in our hearts or in our lives, nor compare with your steadfastness and strength of character which you contributed to our family. We know you have done your part.

Mom we are thankful for your love, your warm smile, your patience and your ever-present listening ear. We especially thank you for the special consideration given to us. Our lives are touched by your faithfulness and high aspiration for us. Your life challenged us to make wise use of our time, as well as our abilities to seek truth and righteousness, to aspire greatly, to love cheerfully, and to take God as our Heavenly Father.

Amen!

You will be forever missed!

Saymon, Jr. Gertie, Charles, Belvin, and her loving baby, Carolyn.

“THE FATHER OF THE JEFFERSON CLAN”

Mr. Saymon Jefferson Sr.

The greatest man I know! If we (speaking for all) had to choose an action hero, let it be known that you are our hero!

You are the father that we believed could do “ANYTHING.” You are a strong, independent, patient, lover of your family, and giver that has ever been known. I often hear you say “Why can’t y’all all get along?”

You have shown us all how to have good work ethics, and character.

We praise God for your love, your guidance and your life!!!

Proud to call you “DADDY,”

Beverly

A TRIBUTE TO MY HUSBAND

Congratulations on the publishing of your first book. You have always been a great speaker, teacher, leader, helper, motivator, and mentor which has enabled you to be a great storyteller. Therefore, there are people that want to hear what you have to say. I have watched you teach our kids and grandkids. All of them, along with myself appreciates and cherish those moments.

Thank you for being the voice that we needed during those times. I have always believed in you and the things that you stand for. There will always be something to do, more things to learn and there will be more stories to tell. I pray that you continue to grow in your endeavors. Remember to keep God first in everything you do.

Love You!

Deborah H. Jefferson

A TRIBUTE TO MY DAD

Integrity, honor, and faith, are just a few words that come to mind when I think of my father. He is a leader, pillar of strength, a man of courage, and charisma who has overcome life's unforeseen obstacles. His work ethic is endless and his top priorities are God, family and career. It is an honor to call Charles Jefferson my father.

To say I am proud of my dad is an understatement. He was a top athlete during his high school years and later received a full scholarship to McNeese State University where he became a record holder. After four years of playing at McNeese State, the Denver Broncos drafted him. This was his ultimate achievement and a dream come true as a football player and as a son.

It's every man's vision to be able to touch thousands of souls. Unknowingly, he inspired thousands of young males who wanted to play football professionally. He was blessed with the opportunity to be a positive role model both on and off the field. As a result, he motivated adolescents in the community to not only follow their dreams, but to never give up regardless of any obstacles. He left behind a legacy as a great athlete, a great family man, a Christian, and a kind and heartfelt man.

I want to thank my father for being present throughout my life and for instilling in me the qualities of a great man. He has made himself available in every way possible-both when needed and not. He did an outstanding job raising my brother and I and we are forever grateful for the priceless wisdom that has was passed down to us. He was hard, stern, and strict, but at the same, he was understanding, caring and compassionate. He pushed us to reach beyond the stars-there were no limits. He taught us the importance of hard work and discipline, being the head of the household, the ability to keep striving and the plan to make strategic goals. Structure and organization were two key determinates of becoming a man. He was our biggest critic, but at the same time, he was our number one fan. He showed us how to be real men.

He is a man that stands on his word and faith in God-he is no doubt, my hero. Not a fictional hero, but my real-life hero. Someone I can see, touch, follow, admire, and most of all, call "DAD." To me, it takes a man of dignity to be a father. He is my friend, disciplinarian, and spiritual leader. In today's society, there's a shortage or misconception of what a father is and should be. To sum up who my father is to me, I have listed several attributes using the acronym

C-H-A-R-L-E-S:

C – Courageous

H – Heroic

A – Articulate

R – Reliable

L – Leader

E – Enthusiastic

S – Strength

Congratulations, dad on all your accomplishments and those to come!
I am forever proud of you…

Sincerely,

Brandon Jefferson

NOT ONE WORD GONE UNSPOKEN-SON TRIBUTE

As I reflect in brief moments of gratitude, love and respect towards my father, it's truly an honor to express my appreciation as a father, mentor, patriarch and now established author. As an African American father, you have always been a man of moral character and family, in which you've stood on firmly. I've watched you grow and change for the better in every way. Since I was a young child, I've watched your desire and passion for knowledge. It never ceased to amaze me, you've inspired us all.

You have done what many say is impossible. You've made believers out of me. You have raised two children into men. Sometimes my brother and I didn't understand why you were so hard on us. Those life lessons and tough love impacted our lives and enriched our minds. You've always been a man of truth and courage. Not once have you ever asked me or Brandon time to be you. All you asked, is that we be the best men we can, and live up to our greatest potential. This is what I admire about you the most. It's truly been a blessing to accompany you on your journey and I pray that God continues to use you as a vessel to be a blessing in the lives of many more.

Let your story be told in admiration and not one word gone unspoken.

God Bless!

Love,

Bryan Jefferson

Paw Paw,
We are extremely proud of your success and the publication of your second book. You have definitely set the standards high. We look forward to one day continuing your legacy. You are our hero and inspiration and we pray that God continues to be
a blessing upon you.

We love you always,

Brooklyn Ann Jefferson and Melani Rose Jefferson

Father-in-law,
Congratulations on all of your achievements, especially the success of our book. You are a man full of wisdom, knowledge, faith, inventiveness, and a man whom I respect dearly. You are truly one of a kind. Continue to be a mentor to us all. You
deserve nothing but the best and with God, you have shown that anything in life is possible. You have always risen to the occasion and play an integral role in your family lives. You are the true definition of a hardworking, dependable father, husband, grandfather, and friend.
Again, congratulations!

Sincerely,
Dr. Melinda J. Jefferson

A GRANDSON'S TRIBUTE

It would be remiss of me not to speak of "teachable moments" I shared with my mother's parents, Willie and Lonnie Magee. While growing up as a young lad, my siblings and I along with mom and dad, would visit our grandparents, sometimes twice a month, during the summer but not so often during the school year. Firstly, my grandmother Lonnie, while she was alive, would leave me with many memorable moments to live by for a lifetime. Here is a brief description of the beauty of my grandmother. She stood about four-foot something tall. She was medium to dark complexion, silky-soft skin, and had hair that was long, thick, black, and beautiful. She was an awesome "woman of God," who loved going to church to praise and worship among friends and family as often as she could. She was a good wife and mother too. I later learned from my mom that my grandmother read novels. She had a smile that could light up a room in a moment's notice. Yes, that was my grandmother whom I loved so dearly. I cannot begin to express how much my grandparents meant to me in every way possible. Now, I would like to share some fond and teachable moments my grandmother instilled in me as a young lad. When it came to hygiene, she would always stress to us kids the importance of keeping your teeth clean and breath fresh no matter what. Also, clean underwear was a must– no exceptions. We were to always wear clean socks and do not forget about your shoes. When bathing, she taught us to always wash behind our ears, underneath our arm pits, and everywhere else that matters. I think you know what I mean! In closing, thank you grandmother for the love and contributions you made in my life for all the right reasons.

Sincerely,

your Grandson Charles Ray Jefferson.

Ok, moving along as it pertains to my grandfather. He, too, provided me with many teachable and fond moments to share for a lifetime. You see, my grandfather, in his own right, was quite a physical specimen. He stood about 6 feet 5 inches tall and weighed between 250– 300 pounds. He was blessed with beautiful (red-bone) skin, best I can remember. Don't mind saying so myself, he was a handsome man (in his own right) and a good husband and father who loved his wife and children tremendously. My grandfather was an excellent farmer of many things such as: watermelons, butter beans, okra, corn, various fruit-trees, etc. He was also a great provider for his family, I might add. According to my mother, my grandfather Willie, was one heck of an athlete in his heyday. Many felt that he was good enough to have played professional baseball if he wanted to. According to many sources, he could hit a baseball out of site and throw one (to use an old expression) a country mile. Wow, I am convinced he really was that good. He also loved going to church with his family, loved helping people, and loved his grandchildren. These are a few things he taught me growing up as a young lad. First; how to skip rocks across a fish pond. Now, that was cool. Secondly, how to know when a watermelon is ripe for the pickings. Thirdly, how to draw fresh well-water from a well in the ground. Need I say more about my grandfather? I could but I think it is best I stop and close out here.

Good times come and go but the memories will last a lifetime. Thanks for the memories, grandfather from the bottom of my heart.

Sincerely,

Your grandson,

Charles Ray Jefferson

MY "BABY" BROTHER

I am so excited about you new endeavor! You have always exceeded any expectations you have set out to do, and I so admire that about you. You are, and have always been unstoppable!!!! Your passion is what persuades others. If I had one word to describe you it would be "SUCCESSFUL." I watched you from childhood, using your talents and abilities to conquer and overcome many obstacles you were faced with. I've witnessed you push yourself to amazing limits, your intelligence, and your drive. Your winning attitude has granted you some of life's greatest success.

This is only the beginning, for I believe that "THE BEST IS YET TO COME."

I can't wait to see what's next!

I LOVE YOU, I'm proud of you and I'm here for you.

P.S. This is only a launching pad…. God has something even greater than this is store for you! Mom prayed for you, she encouraged you, and she believed in you!!! So soarrrrrrrr!

Affectionately,

Your sister, Beverly

A TRIBUTE TO MY BROTHER-IN-LAW

Congratulations, Charles on the writing of your book. You have been an amazing brother-in-law since marring my sister, Deborah. You have made yourself available to lend a hand whenever anyone in the family needs you, particularly our mother, Elnora Henderson Price. As you know, I have been disabled for the past four years and being the only boy, I am unable to do the things for her that she needs me to do. You jumped right in where I left off and now helps her with anything that she needs, which is such a blessing to me since neither of us are able to. I can say that I truly look at you as a brother and not a brother in-law. Continued success in the next chapter of your life.

Eddie C. Henderson (Aka Man)

Pictured: McNeese State University plaque, 1978

Pictured: My big brother and I sharing a jubilant moment

Pictured: Back of the Spanish American Landmark

Pictured: Spanish American Landmark

I actually climbed it several times during my early adolescent years.

Pictured: Me on the second row, #32.

Pictured: Junior High Photo, row number three from left to right, # 32.

Pictured: (left to right) Saymon Jr.,
Belvin, and yours truly.

Pictured: Hall of Fame coffee mug

CHARLES JEFFERSON

Charles has played defensive halfback for the Golden Lions for three years. He is the son of Mrs. Arcenia Jefferson and holds membership in Student Government and belongs to State Temple Church.

Pictured: Me on left running back #32 with my teammates.

Pictured: My dearest Mom

Picture: One-On-One with Bo - Chas

Want to Play?

Body Measurements:

Waist Size 32”
Height 6 ft. 0”
Weight 190 Lbs.
Wing Span 76” or 6 ft. 4”
Hand Size 9”
Neck size 18”
High I.Q on and off the football field
Thigh Size 33-1/2”
Shoe Size 11”
Forty-Time 4.5 second
Vertical Jump 36”
Defensive Half-Back
Extraordinary flexibility

Pictured: Me on the field prior to my junior year campaign

Pictured: Mom, your love for your family will radiate through the end of time.

Pictured: Sister Gertie and daughter Latrenda

Pictured: My sisters Gertie and Belvin came to help me celebrate my 23rd birthday in Houston.

Pictured: My father, Saymon Jefferson Sr.
WW II Veteran Years of Service 1943-47

Charlie Jefferson

A call from Denver

Pictured: Me receiving the draft call

Pictured: Jefferson gains altitude after fumble recovery

Pictured: Another football stadium that reveal many secrets to my success

Pictured: Holiday photo of little sister, Belvin at home

Pictured: My mother, Missionary Evangelist, Arcenia Magee Jefferson. Thank you, Mom, for your love and those sweet words of encouragement to live by.

Baby boy,

"Charles Ray"

HALL OF FAME
CHARLES JEFFERSON
FOOTBALL
1976-1978
M
McNEESE STATE

Pictured: Myself during my senior year campaign

Eye-of-the-tiger

“Time to Hunt ”

Pictured: My father in his chair at home relaxing

37
#37
#37

Pictured: left to right:
1976 Independence-Bowl Ring
1975-High School Graduation Ring
2014-Football Hall of Fame Ring

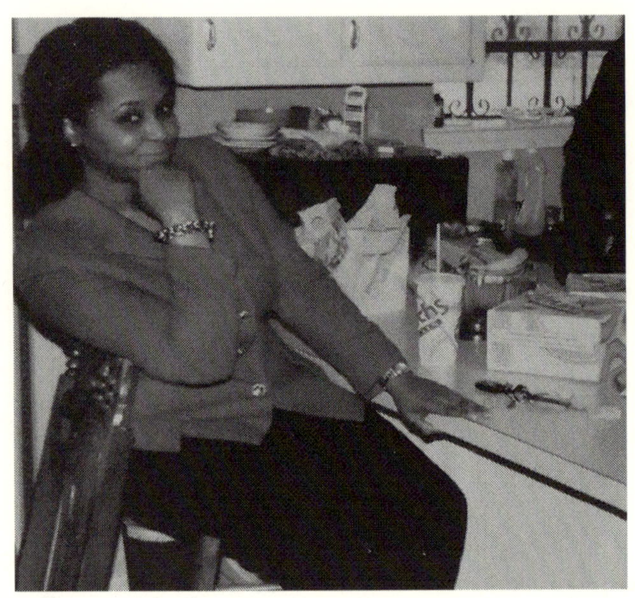

Pictured: My baby sister, Carolyn Jefferson Porche,
on a bar stool at the counter having a cold drink and a bite of bird.

Pictured: My baby sister, Carolyn, and my uncle Lawrence.

Pictured: My dad leaving his parked truck.

Thank you for the love and sacrifices you made for our family!

Love you, Pops.

Baby boy,

Charles Ray

Pictured: This indicates a prolific accomplishment I attained during my tenure at McNeese State University: 50th Anniversary Southland Conference Plaque

Pictured: My 1976 Independence- Bowl plaque.

Pictured: A Silver-plated belt buckle gifted to me by The Houston Oilers Organization in 1980.

Pictured: My baby sister, Carolyn, celebrating another milestone birthday with family and friends.

Love,

Your baby brother,

Charles Ray

Pictured: A collection of my Hall of Fame moments

Acceptance Speech Preparation

The time had come for me to prepare my acceptance speech. It took 2-3 weeks to nail it. I would like to acknowledge the fact that I wrote my own acceptance speech. However, I would like to thank my niece, Latrenda Lee Jefferson, for the proper editorial and presentation format. She put forth the effort and excelled.

Kudos to Latrenda

What Does Being in the Hall of Fame Mean to Me?

For me, being in the Hall of Fame means that all my hard work, dedication, and sacrifice paid off. It is the ultimate praise a player can receive in any sport on any level.

I would like to thank McNeese State University, the Hall of Fame committee, coaching staff, teammates, team doctors, training staff, fans, the media, and the city of Lake Charles for having my family and me here today. This is truly an honor and a special privilege to be nominated for such a prestigious award. Please know that your selection of me for the 2014 class will always be cherished and remembered.

It would be very remiss of me not to mention the names of a few collegiate teammates of mine who since passed away. These individuals helped make this special moment in my life come true. Their names are as follows: Mitch Tyson, Kent Mudd, Raymond Martin, Artie Shankle, and Mike McArthur.

Goooooo Cowboys!

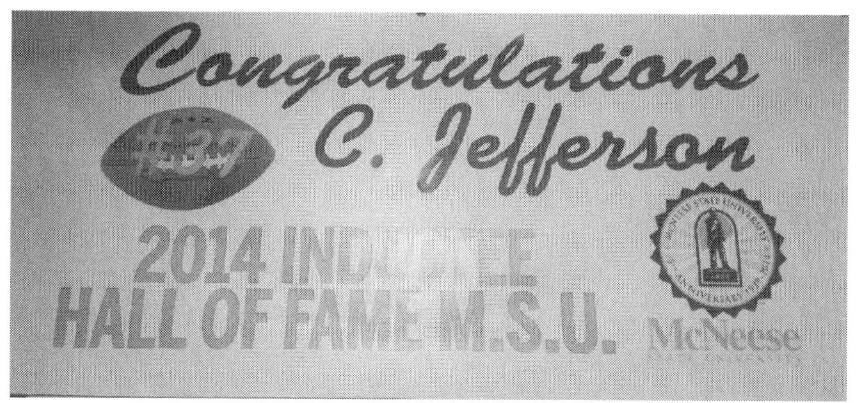

My Hall of Fame Speech

Good afternoon, everyone. First and foremost, I would like to thank my Heavenly Father who made this moment in my life possible. I had never imagined that I would be honored alongside such an amazing group of men, and it is truly awesome that I get to share it with you all. I would like to take time to thank my family, mainly my mother, father, and siblings for their immeasurable love and support. I would like to thank my wife, Deborah, my daughter, D'Andra, and my sons Brandon, Bryan, and Eric. Finally, I would like to give a special thank you to all my family members and friends present here today and those who could not be here. When I look back, I fondly remember my coach at Capitol High School, Roman Bates Jr., and McNeese's personal scout and coach Moe O'Brien who was sent to Capitol High to meet with Coach Bates to assess my skills as a collegiate football player, the late Moe O'Brien. My old high school didn't have much film of me to share, only two years of special team stats and a scrimmage game or two. I can't thank Coach Bates enough. He used his convincing and encouraging words to Coach Moe about me. Coach Moe then spoke to McNeese's Jack Doland and Ernie Duplechin. It only took five plays for them to be convinced that "This kid is a player. We need to sign him." By the way, McNeese was university most invested in my full football scholarship.

About the Author

Charles Ray Jefferson was born May 5, 1957, in New Orleans, Louisiana. He was raised in Baton Rouge. He is the third child of Arcenia and Saymon Jefferson, Sr. He was educated in the East Baton Rouge Parish Public School system where he attended Reddy Elementary, McKinley Junior High School, Istrouma Junior High School and graduated from Capitol Senior High School. During early high school years, his skill as an effective defensive back was stifled by a right ankle fracture during a jamboree football game. This was a practice game that lasted approximately 20–30 minutes.

Charles was offered a football scholarship to McNeese State University in 1975 where he studied Radio-Television and Education. During his four-year collegiate career, Charles played in the first-ever Independence-Bowl in Shreveport, Louisiana. In 1976 he finished with twenty career interceptions to his credit, became a three-time All-Southland Conference (SLC) defensive back, and earned Honorable Mention All-American with three different sporting magazines. In the Spring of 1979, Charles was drafted by the Denver Broncos in the fourth-round, becoming the first African American football player from McNeese State University, to be drafted to play in the National Football League (NFL). Charles went on to enjoy three years with the Denver Broncos and Houston Oilers.

Once his professional football career concluded, he returned home to Baton Rouge, Louisiana where he worked for Leon Picard Chevrolet as a new car salesperson for approximately 1.5 years. Next, he ventured into a new career field as a courier/salesperson with Emery Worldwide Courier Service for nearly three years and embarked on a new job career with Fisher Service Company as an Instrument Control Valve Technician for 20 years. Again, the time had come for Charles to move on. This time he accepted a position with Westgate Instrumentation and Electrical Group at Dow Chemical in Plaquemine, Louisiana as a Gas Monitor/ PH-Water Treatment Technician for 3.5

years. Afterward, Charles returned to a position of enjoyment. In September of 2012, Charles became employed with Satsuma Controls and Valves as a Control Valve Technician. After four years with Satsuma, Charles resigned due to a medical condition. Nearly 35 years later, Charles was nominated for induction into the McNeese State University Football Hall of Fame Class of 2014. Charles was also added to the SLC's 1970 All-Decade Football Team. He was later named to the ALL- 75th Defensive Back Team.

Charles has since retired. However, it hasn't kept him from pursuing his future ventures such as author, researcher, and songwriter. He continues to strive to define his legacy in his Lord and Savior, Jesus.

Made in the USA
Coppell, TX
27 January 2022

72452588R10081